WRITING
TO MAKE
AN IMPACT

WRITING TO MAKE AN IMPACT

EXPANDING THE VISION OF WRITING IN THE SECONDARY CLASSROOM

Sandra Murphy
Mary Ann Smith

TEACHERS COLLEGE PRESS

TEACHERS COLLEGE | COLUMBIA UNIVERSITY
NEW YORK AND LONDON

national writing project

BERKELEY, CA

Published simultaneously by Teachers College Press,® 1234 Amsterdam Avenue, New York, NY 10027 and National Writing Project, 2120 University Avenue, Berkeley, CA 94704

Through its mission, the National Writing Project (NWP) focuses the knowledge, expertise, and leadership of our nation's educators on sustained efforts to help youth become successful writers and learners. NWP works in partnership with local Writing Project sites, located on nearly 200 university and college campuses, to provide high-quality professional development in schools, universities, libraries, museums, and after-school programs. NWP envisions a future where every person is an accomplished writer, engaged learner, and active participant in a digital, interconnected world.

Cover design by Patricia Palao.

An excerpt from the poem "At the airport-security checkpoint . . ." from *Don't Let Me Be Lonely: An American Lyric* by Claudia Rankine is reprinted with the permission of The Permissions Company, LLC on behalf of Graywolf Press, graywolfpress.org. Copyright © 2004 by Claudia Rankine.

Library of Congress Cataloging-in-Publication Data is available at loc.gov

ISBN 978-0-8077-6396-4 (paper)
ISBN 978-0-8077-6397-1 (hardcover)
ISBN 978-0-8077-7860-9 (ebook)

Printed on acid-free paper
Manufactured in the United States of America

The point of writing is to have something to say and to make a difference in saying it. Rarely, however, is impact the focus in writing instruction in English class.

—*Grant Wiggins*

Contents

Contents

Acknowledgments

Since the beginnings of the Bay Area Writing Project in 1974, we have looked inside our profession to where the action is—the classrooms of committed, courageous teachers—for informed approaches and challenging questions, for experiments and discoveries and mind-stretching conversations. Throughout our teaching and writing lives, we've had the privilege to learn from colleagues whose work has inspired and nudged us to do more, to reach higher, to do better, to think harder.

We had so much support and goodwill as we were writing this book. These friends and colleagues, in particular, gave us generous amounts of time and wise counsel:

The teachers whose classroom practices and wisdom we feature in this book. We are grateful for all the hours you spent with us, for answering our endless questions, and for giving us brilliant models of *writing to make an impact*: Rebekah Caplan, Matt Colley, Laury Fischer, Hayley Hill, Judy Kennedy, Bill Kirby, Brooke McWilliams, Stan Pesick, Emma Richardson, Hillary Walker.

Our teaching colleagues in the Bay Area Writing Project Writing Group. We are indebted to you for reading big chunks of this book and giving us emphatic suggestions about how to improve our own writing: Laury Fischer, Grace Morizawa, Stan Pesick, Meredith Pike-Baky, Greta Volmer, Hillary Walker, Shelly Weintraub.

Behind-the-scenes advisors. Thank you to the friends we constantly pestered as we refined our concept for this book. You helped us think through our ideas, pointed out resources, and encouraged us to shift gears when we were stuck or going in a questionable direction: Robin Atwood, Young Wan Choi, Tom Fox, Linda Friedrich, Barbara Heenan, Susan Marks, Mark St. John, Sherry Swain, Susan Threatt.

National Writing Project teachers. Your insights travel widely and the work you do every day matters beyond measure. Jim Gray would be so proud of what the Writing Project he invented has become.

CHAPTER 1

Writing to Make an Impact

You know the moment—when everything you have ever believed as a teacher plays out in front of you. Your students shine, even if briefly, and there it is.

Here's one of our moments: We were sitting in on a full day of presentations by 100 high schoolers who had just finished their civic action projects dealing with social issues. They gathered in a local hotel, wearing their best clothes and trying to hide their nerves behind giddy smiles and sometimes fleeting eye contact. Even though they carried with them impressive illustrations of their work—videos, posters, PowerPoints, photos, graphics—they were on the spot. After all, what could be more daunting than talking to peers, most of whom they didn't even know?

Toward the end of the day, the participants voted on the "best" presentation for a rerun. The group of students who held the winning card stood nervously in front of the large audience and began with a compelling backstory about themselves. Each had some personal connection to teen pregnancy, a friend or family member whose future dramatically changed because of an unexpected baby. But, they explained, the topic was too cavernous for their civic action project. So they decided to zero in on what goes on during health class at their school. Did this required class address teen pregnancy? The answer was "no." The four students, now curious and more committed than ever, went online to check out whether health classes even existed in all high schools in all states. Again, the answer was "no."

As their research and writeup took shape, they became advocates for responsible education when it comes to a critical health concern like teen pregnancy. "Otherwise," one of them noted, "you know where kids get their information. From each other. In the halls. From urban myths. From rumors."

You couldn't miss how animated and "on" these students were. Something was happening. The audience of peers—even at the end of a long day—was with them, heads nodding. As for the adults in the room, we were probably thinking alike: Wouldn't it be nice if all writing opportunities brought down the house this way?

We are not the only teachers who have asked themselves this question. University of California, Berkeley, professor Scott Saul (2018) has done his own soul searching:

I'd started to feel a sense of diminishing returns when I simply asked students to produce what has long been the "industry standard" in English departments: the five-page essay of close analysis. At its best, this assignment allowed students to shine new light on a formerly obscure corner of a text (and prove to themselves that they were ready for the rigors of graduate study in the discipline). At its worst, this assignment felt like make-work to students—something written only for the eyes of the person grading their writing. It was inconceivable, to many, that anyone else might be interested in their thoughts on, say, Emily Dickinson or Robert Louis Stevenson or Toni Morrison. They were writing an essay because they had to, for someone who was reading it because *he* had to—not exactly a recipe for the production of deathless prose. (para. 2)

Though analyzing literature, writing reports, or creating arguments may equip young writers with important thinking and writing skills, too many traditional school writing assignments stay strictly within the boundaries of the "industry standard." Here's how Kelly Gallagher (2006) puts it:

One reason students don't write well is that they do not care what they are writing about. If you think about it, we often ask students to do the kind of writing that we, as adults, *never* do. When was the last time you sat down at home and wrote a draft analyzing Shakespeare's use of biblical allusions in *Hamlet*? Or wrote a letter that aligned perfectly to a rigid, five-paragraph format? It seems to me that we spend a lot of time preparing students for "fake writing"—the kinds of writing they will never do once they leave school. (p. 90)

WRITING THAT MATTERS

If we agree that not all writing is created equal, then the question is: What kind of writing lands somewhere in the top tier, at least where young writers are concerned? One answer comes from the Stanford Study of Writing, which began in September 2001 and included 189 students over a period of 5 years. Author Cathy Davidson (2017) writes about this study in some detail. A key finding will probably not surprise you. Students "do not do particularly well in writing papers just for the sake of writing papers. Rather, students value writing that 'makes something happen in the world'" (p. 93):

> The overwhelming majority of Americans will not write academic papers for a living.
> —Grant Wiggins

In the typical five-paragraph essay, for example, the writer employs a prescribed method, almost a formula, to shape each section of the essay, and you don't deviate from that structure even if your audience changes. Nor do you need to because, in the traditional five-paragraph essay, the audience is unchanging: it's the professor. Students learn to write essays that only they and their professor will be reading, in a form and format that are rarely used beyond the classroom. (p. 93)

We notice, as you probably do, that the five-paragraph essay often emerges as the villain. Certainly, it is one of the most deeply rooted structures in all of school writing. We would argue that writing can mean so much more to students when it breaks out of old, tired molds, regardless of the number of paragraphs.

We have it on good authority that many kids—and, for that matter, many teachers—agree:

A large group of college students participating in a research study were asked, "What is good writing?" The researchers expected fairly straightforward answers like "writing that gets its message across," but the students kept coming back to one central idea: At some point during your college years or soon after, you are highly likely to create writing that is not just something that you turn in for a grade, but writing that you do because you want to make a difference. The writing that matters most to many students and citizens, then, is writing that has an effect in the world: writing that gets up off the page or screen, puts on its working boots, and marches out to get something done! (Lunsford, 2011, p. 890)

> The writing that matters most is . . . writing that gets up off the page or screen, puts on its working boots, and marches out to get something done!
> —Andrea Lunsford

We are definitely on board with writing that marches and sings and exists because there is something for it to do. We imagine most teachers want the writing that comes from their classrooms to carry a tune, to change minds and hearts, to stir up a conversation. So, what does writing look like when it falls under these lively banners?

In this book, we hope to expand the view of what it means for *writing to make an impact*, to throw open the door and invite in all kinds of possibilities. There are obvious examples—ones that people are likely to think of first, like persuasion in all its many forms (essays, petitions, flyers, letters, and so on). But what about narrative and poetry and personal stories? What does it really mean for writing *to do something*?

WRITING THAT GOES PLACES

We know intuitively that writing at its best takes us somewhere, or to borrow the famous words of Dr. Seuss, "Oh, the places [your writing] will go!" (Geisel, 1990). So why not wonder, as we have, how we can make more of the writing in school go places?

For starters, we suggest that *writing to make an impact* has many possible destinations. Consider just a handful of examples.

To:
>   Entertain
>   Console
>   Request
>   Demand
>   Encourage
>   Flatter
>   Question
>   Enlighten
>   Condemn
>   Challenge

We offer this list, not to suggest that students must learn to write for any one of these destinations, but to illustrate that *writing to make an impact* can take off in lots of directions. And then there's the audience. Student writing doesn't really "go places" if it lands solely in the teacher's lap. Besides, it's a back-breaking, merciless job to be the sole guardian of the writing. We assume that you, our colleagues, have experienced, as we have, that moment of truth when students pay attention only to the grade on their writing, not to our perceptive, laboriously crafted, masterful comments. Who wants to be the only audience and responder anyway?

> In real-world "audience" and "purpose" are not mere buzzwords; they are task-defining: the consequences of your writing matter for a specific audience in a specific situation.
> —Grant Wiggins

W*riting to make an impact* might get attention or a laugh, make a clever point, shift someone's thinking, touch an emotion, or offer a new perspective. It can be playful or serious. It can take risks or not. Regardless, the secrets behind it are these:

- The students care about the writing and what it does.
- The writing itself exists to make things happen—well beyond demonstrating some kind of competence.
- The point of the writing is to have an effect on someone or something.

IMPACT IN THE HERE AND NOW

Let's be honest. School writing originates in school, no matter how we dress it up or down. It may wander briefly outside the campus walls, but it always comes back for a grade, or in the best of circumstances, for some kind of learning and sharing. What would it take for school writing to happen in and around school, but to do or be more than traditional school writing?

Writing to make an impact makes contact. It resonates. It inspires or moves or surprises, or convinces, or just plain pleases. As for its place in school, Grant Wiggins (2009) has claimed that it seldom shows up: "*The point of writing is to have something to say and to make a difference in saying it. Rarely, however, is impact the focus in writing instruction in English class*" (p. 29; italics added).

Wiggins suggests that students should be invested *now*, find real reasons for writing while they are learning to write, and most important, have an impact in the present moment. We can't overemphasize this idea of investment. A 2015 Gallup student poll, "Engaged Today: Ready for Tomorrow," revealed that by 12th grade, 66% of students are disengaged. "These students are not involved, have little enthusiasm for school, and do not feel they contribute to the learning environment" (O'Connell & Vandas, 2016, para. 2).

When it comes to writing, teachers can create investment opportunities for students by showing them that their writing counts, that it can make some kind of difference, even in school, especially if its purpose is to "cause a fuss." Perhaps Wiggins (2009) says it best: ". . . the point [of writing] is to open the mind or heart of a real audience—cause a fuss, achieve a feeling, start some kind of thinking. . . ." (p. 30).

The excerpt below exemplifies what it means to "achieve a feeling," or "start some kind of thinking." It dramatizes a crisis on an airplane and takes us into the pilot's head. It sets us up for the unexpected: that expert piloting is as much about improvising and multitasking as it is about working the controls.

In his bestselling book *Outliers: The Story of Success*, Malcolm Gladwell (2008) writes about what pilots need to know so they can communicate in a crisis. He tells the story of veteran Sri Lankan pilot Suren Ratwatte, who experienced an urgent situation in a plane he was flying from Dubai. One of the passengers in the back was having what flight attendants thought was a stroke. The plane was still full of fuel and too heavy to land with the automated landing system. Though Ratwatte knew he could dump the fuel, he weighed the consequences: ". . . countries hate it when you dump fuel. It's messy stuff and they would have routed me somewhere over the Baltic Sea and it would have taken me forty minutes and the lady probably would have died. So I decided to land anyway. My choice."

> At that stage, I took over the controls. . . . I had to ensure that the airplane touched down very softly, otherwise, there would have been the risk of structural damage. It could have been a real mess. . . . It was a lot of work. You're juggling a lot of balls. You've got to get it right. I'd never been to Helsinki before. I had no idea how the airport was, no idea whether the runways were long enough. I had to find an approach. . . . At one point I was talking to three different people—talking to Dubai, talking to MedLink, which is a service in Arizona where they put a doctor on call,

and I was talking to the two doctors who were attending to the lady in the back. It was nonstop for forty minutes. (p. 190)

Obviously, Ratwatte had to have excellent piloting skills. Author Gladwell (2008) points out that he had to balance the probability of plane damage in relation to a woman's life, and he had to come up to speed quickly about the requirements of a foreign airport. But most important, in 40 minutes, he had to talk to everyone concerned, including the copilot, doctors, passengers, managers in Dubai, and airport personnel in Helsinki.

> What was required of Ratwatte was that he *communicate*, and communicate not just in the sense of issuing commands, but also in the sense of encouraging and cajoling and calming and negotiating and sharing information in the clearest and most transparent manner possible. (p. 192)

What is it about this story that makes it have some kind of impact on the reader? The subject is inherently interesting and personally relevant for many readers—what goes on behind that locked metal door to the cockpit, particularly in an emergency. We definitely want to believe that our pilots are supremely gifted men and women who can pull everything together at a moment's notice. Gladwell re-creates the tension of this flight by letting us hear, in the pilot's words, what was at stake. The risks. The split-second decisions. Odds are that readers will pull for the pilot and passengers to land safely.

The story also dramatizes the need for superior leadership and communication skills that go beyond knowing how to fly and land a plane. Gladwell (2008) tells us, "Every major airline now has what is called 'Crew Resource Management' training, which is designed to teach junior crew members how to communicate clearly and assertively" (p. 197).

This writing exists to make something happen. It entertains, enlightens, and engages the reader. It is not a research paper, a book report, or a report of information. It is not regurgitation of what other written sources have to say. Certainly, Gladwell did his reading, but he also talked to live people who shared their experiences and expertise with him. So we, the readers, feel like we are on the inside track.

WRITING IN THE "REAL WORLD"

For today's students, "real-world" writing is often self-sponsored. Whatever form it takes on social media, it happens in the moment and it invites a reaction. It's what Kathleen Yancey (2009) calls "new composing"—writing with the intention of sharing, encouraging dialogue, and participating (p. 5). Our idea of *writing to make an impact* is in line with this new composing. We want to encourage young writers to write with intention (their own) so that their writing might influence, touch, sway, or dazzle, whatever their intention might be.

Ken Lindblom (2015) argues that social media offer the real deal when it comes to writing:

> Some may scoff at the significance of social media, but when students write on social media they are devising something to say, considering how best to say it to their intended audience, and they . . . either see that they are understood or they must rewrite it, so they are understood. . . . This is *real* writing (para. 3).

We might add here that if students are invested in their writing as it shows up on social media, then "narrowly prescribed school writing"—to use Kelly Gallagher's (2011) phrase (p. 7)—is likely to seem doubly boring and pointless.

Mourning the schoolishness of school, professor of education Anne Elrod Whitney (2011) looks back on her own school experience: "So much of what happens in school has always seemed . . . well, fake" (p. 51). Yet Whitney acknowledges, as we do, that literacy activities—no matter how we decorate them with "real-world" purposes and audiences— still take place in a school context. She suggests asking a critical question about whatever activities we devise: "What are their [students'] purposes for undertaking this activity?" (p. 61).

> I don't believe that all classroom writing activities have to connect directly to the real world. The important thing is that the activity has a significance or personal value for the learners and that they know why they're doing it.
> —David Barton

"Real-world" writing, then, needs to be more than a facsimile of writing that lives outside of school and roams around in the lives of adults. Knowing how to make a claim to an insurance company or a complaint to the city council about the potholes on your street is important, for sure. But real-worldliness also means bringing into the classroom the real world of our students—their purposes, their frameworks of engagement and participation. *Writing to make an impact* veers away from schoolishness by opening up opportunities for students to use the skills and habits of mind they display when they create an online presence.

EXPANDING THE VISION OF WRITING IN SCHOOL

In 2004, the National Endowment for the Arts funded a writing project called Operation Homecoming: Writing the Wartime Experience. The purpose was to help U.S. troops in Afghanistan and Iraq and their loved ones give words to their wartime experiences. According to "Soldiers' Stories" in *The New Yorker* (June 12, 2006), 6,000 troops participated, producing "more than ten thousand pages of writing—nonfiction, fiction, and poetry" (para. 1).

The men and women who were part of this project attended writing workshops led by distinguished American writers. *The New Yorker* (2006) reports: "They were told to write freely, without fear of official constraints or oversight" (para. 1).

In the end, the writing became part of an anthology and a Library of Congress archive as well as the inspiration for two award-winning documentaries.

Indeed, the Operation Homecoming writing made a sizable impact, in this case, on the veterans and their families (those who are doing the writing); on readers and film watchers; and on the cause of helping those who serve our country to heal.

Former National Writing Project director Richard Sterling (2006) notes:

> [What they wrote] is a powerful tribute to what happens when people are invited to write and to tell their stories. . . . Providing such opportunities to write—whether to soldiers returning home from war or families recovering from a natural disaster—seems to be a welcome and accepted part of our culture. But I don't have to tell all of you that it has been a challenge to make the vision of writing in school match the broader vision of writing out of school. (para. 6 & 7)

So much of Operation Homecoming speaks to our purpose. We, too, hope to make the long-held vision of school writing broader and, like Operation Homecoming, more connected to life stories and issues, insights and calls for action. We are not rejecting the "required" kinds of writing. We have taught them all—from literary analysis to argument—and would still fight for the right to do so. That said, we recognize that much of the writing that students do in school has two main goals: to show what they know or to show what they can do. And yet, there are classroom teachers everywhere who take writing one more step. They invite students to do something with their writing, to use it to make an impact—on a cause, on a reader, on themselves. We also recognize that writing in the 21st century is more public, potentially more influential, and richer in possibilities than ever before. Writing streams and tweets and pops up daily on screens all over the world. This is writing that "goes places," as Dr. Seuss would say. What better time to give wings to the writing our students do in school?

> Language, particularly its written form, has shaped our world, it has changed our world, and it has been the first instrument of change.
> —Richard Sterling

CLASSROOM CLOSEUPS

To start this book, we talked to secondary and community college teachers—most, but not all, National Writing Project (NWP) teachers. We selected 12 teachers whose work exemplified that extra step, the idea of *writing to make an impact*. We asked them to tell us what they do in the classroom and why they do it. In some instances, we talked to their students about their experiences. The writing from these classrooms runs the gamut, including poetry and narrative, petitions and proposals, emails to others, and reflections to self.

Our stories about teachers take the form of what we call "classroom close-ups." Their purpose is to illustrate how teachers create the conditions for students to do something with their writing. Each closeup features teaching ideas and teacher commentary. In each of the closeups, students have opportunities to do many of the following:

- Learn new ways to write
- Tell their own stories
- Select issues that matter to them
- Keep a reader firmly in mind
- Broaden the audience for their writing beyond the teacher
- Make an impact

We start Chapter 2, "Getting Your Mojo" with a pitch for giving students the background, confidence, and know-how for writing well. Both of the classroom closeups illustrate how students try out new writing skills and new ways of thinking about their communities, and at the same time, develop the ability to assume a public voice, to weave in personal stories, and to communicate with elected officials, newspaper editors, and a general audience.

In Chapter 3, "Writing Your Narrative," we focus on personal narrative—a starting point for and the heart of so much of writing that has a noticeable effect on a reader and, often, the writer, too. In some ways, the power of narrative to make an impact needs no explanation. It stands out in the student writing in this chapter. Both the classroom closeups and the teaching playbook feature strategies for giving narrative that extra zing to go beyond a simple recounting of an incident for a classroom assignment.

In Chapter 4, "Writing for Poetic Effect," we make the case that when students experiment with poetic language, they learn how to use words, phrases, and sentences more effectively, not just for writing poetry, but for all kinds of prose as well. Poetry, unlike so many other genres, gives students the chance to play with language, and in the process, to add new "portable" skills to their repertoires. Poetry also offers opportunities for students to bring their lives outside of school into the writing they do on the inside.

Chapter 5, "Writing to Take Action," features a single classroom closeup packed with techniques for using writing in a civic engagement project. In this case, students learn how to respond responsibly and powerfully to the social forces around them. Civic engagement writing challenges students to be precise and accurate, to make an effective case, to use a public voice, and to reach outside the classroom for an audience. It's here that we also introduce eight students who talk frankly about their experiences working together on a chosen issue and their efforts to create awareness and change.

In Chapter 6, "Writing to Figure Things Out," students reflect on their work by writing about what they take away from participating in long-term projects, often including their challenges, processes, and questions. The impact of reflective writing is on the writer, with a side benefit for teachers, who gain insights into their students' thinking. The classroom closeups and the teaching playbook highlight strategies for supporting students as they look back and learn from their accomplishments and challenges.

Chapter 7, "Writing to Think Critically," brings together narrative, civic action, collaboration, and reflection in the Proteus Project—a first-person research project in which students select their topic, investigate it, engage in a participatory experience, and, most important, think critically about their topic instead of merely reporting on it. A second research project, this time from a history class, invites students to find a moment in the past that intrigues them and bring it to life, including the human drama that surrounded it. In the process, they pose and address a critical question.

A note about the hashtags you will find under the headings and subheadings in this book. We use them to draw attention and to organize, not to mention to have fun. We've read that "tweets that use hashtags get twice as much engagement as those that don't. Tweets with more than two hashtags saw engagement drop by 17%. Perhaps because too many hashtags look spammy" (Brooks, 2014, para. 14). In addition to whatever role hashtags play in the world or in this book, we are inspired by teachers like Hillary Walker, who has her students create hashtags to capture the essence of whatever article they are reading at the moment. You can find out more about Walker in Chapter 6.

TEACHING PLAYBOOK

In addition to the classroom closeups, each chapter includes a teaching playbook—three or four short exercises that give students manageable practice in areas such as making judgments about writing, trying out writing strategies that work, engaging a reader, gathering resources, managing long-term projects, and reflecting on their learning. In many instances, their benefits rest in their repetition, rather than their use as a one-shot activity.

You might recognize the term *playbook*. Businesses use playbooks as a source of activities or "plays" to create better products and services. More familiar is the playbook a sports team relies on in the course of a game. For example, in football, there are running plays to move the ball down the field: *quarterback sneak*, *up the middle*, *end-around*, and *sweep*. On the defensive side, who hasn't heard of *rushing the passer* or *blitzing*?

Playbooks serve as a guide. Likewise, our playbooks are not recipes or lesson plans to be diligently followed. If a sports team ran the same plays the same way in every game, it would be at a disadvantage. Instead, a great sports team adjusts plays to the situation at hand. Similarly, our teaching playbook serves as a starting point. You can experiment with the plays and adapt them to your needs.

STUDENT WRITING

Throughout the book, we offer examples of students' work that we think makes an impact—on an audience, and also many times on the student writer himself or herself. In most cases, we have chosen top-of-the-line writing to serve as models of what's possible. This poem by a high school senior is a preview of what students can do when they learn the necessary skills and receive the go-ahead to break away from conventional purposes for school writing.

Trade
By Makayla Raby

Daddy smiled
as he stuffed the
rusted trunk full
of green, frayed
suitcases and
plastic Walmart
sacks, double bagged.
He spit out
black sludge
onto the dry,
cracking dirt
and muttered,
"Don't go city
on me, girly."
He grabbed
my pale,
uncovered shoulders
and pulled me
tight against him.
His sweat soaked
my shirt and
I sniffed one
last gulp of him.
Pine, sweat, and beer.
He released me

and I hopped into
the decaying
Buick Century.
Momma slapped on
her sunglasses
and lit up her
cigarette, pulling
onto Highway 15.
I watched as the
trees were traded
for towers, the
flowers for cars,
and the animals
for people.
I took a leap
into a bottomless
unknown and I
traded my
down-home roots
for opportunities
not found amongst
the deer, the trees,
or the flowers.
But I never went
city on him.

Oh, the pictures. The sounds. The smell of a loved one. The memories of saying good-bye. The promises we keep. The trades we make—one life for another. This poem calls up our shared experiences. It creates the conditions for the reader to have an aesthetic and emotional response. Simply put, it makes an impact.

CHAPTER 2

Getting Your Mojo

> To some degree, we're all familiar with Mojo. If you've ever given a speech—
> and done it well—you know the feeling. . . . It might be a sales pitch to a
> customer. It might be an internal presentation where you defend your work
> to your bosses and peers. It might be a eulogy at a loved one's funeral, or
> a toast at your daughter's wedding. Whatever the occasion, if you've done
> it well—if the audience hangs on every word, nods in agreement, laughs
> at your jokes, and applauds at the end. . . . You're firing on all cylinders *and*
> everyone in the room senses it. That is the essence of Mojo. (Goldsmith,
> 2009, p. 4)

ABOUT THIS CHAPTER: BUILDING CONFIDENCE AND
KNOW-HOW FOR WRITING THAT MAKES AN IMPACT

The idea that students might come to a writing task armed with some Mojo
seems to us a prerequisite for all kinds of writing and especially for *writing to
make an impact*. In order to change someone's
mind, propose an idea, call something into
question, provoke a response, or make an audience laugh, gasp, or applaud, writers need all
the confidence and credibility they can get, and
maybe even a touch of cockiness. In this chapter, we will look at what it means to cultivate
Mojo, focusing specifically on helping students
pick up the knowledge they need to "fire on all
cylinders." The two classroom closeups illustrate ways to ease students into new
situations and to introduce new skills so students develop some self-assurance.

> [Mojo] is the moment
> when we do something
> that's purposeful,
> powerful, and positive,
> *and* the rest of the world
> recognizes it.
> —Marshall Goldsmith

MOJO BUILDER #1: UNDERSTANDING THE CONTEXT FOR WRITING
#learnthelandscape #knowwhatsup

When we talk about understanding the context for a piece of writing, we have
in mind that students can answer questions like these:

- What is the purpose for this writing? What is it supposed *to do*?
- Who is the audience? What readers is the writer trying to impact?
- What is the situation? Where is there an opening to make something happen?
- What kinds of writing will best suit this situation?

Before we go into some detail about these questions, let's test out the extent to which the answers matter, whether for writing or for some other life pursuit. Think about the last time you were getting ready to go to a party. What did you want to know before you got there? No doubt you paid attention to the reason for the party (birthday, wedding reception, graduation, and so on). You might have scanned the evite to find out who else would be coming. You probably needed to know when and where to show up, what to bring, what to wear—formal or informal—and maybe whether or not you could bring a guest. In the end, you might have decided to disregard the dress code or to arrive just in time for dessert. Parties, after all, are not job interviews. But for many of us who want to be comfortable and in-the-know socially, understanding the party context makes sense.

When writers are unclear about the context for their work, they waffle around, trying to make decisions. They start to lose confidence. We all know what it looks like when a student writer's Mojo takes a dive because adult writers struggle in the same way when we try to write without a clear sense of what to do: procrastinating. Falling back on a formula or any "easy" way out. Fussing over some distraction like what font to use. Let's face it. Most of us need some direction when it comes to context.

CLASSROOM CLOSEUP:
HELPING WRITERS CONNECT WITH CONTEXT
#trialanderror

Understanding the context for a particular piece of writing doesn't necessarily happen all at once. Most students will not have an epiphany. Even with preparation and ongoing support, students may still have to go through a period of trial and error to nail down how context affects their writing choices.

Teacher Hayley Hill offers an example of what we mean. In tiny Taylorsville, Mississippi (population 1,286), Hayley Hill found a made-to-order situation for her secondary students to write for an audience and purpose beyond the classroom. Each year, Taylorsville holds an annual fundraiser for the American Cancer Society, which comes with advance publicity to energize and motivate the community. For Hill, everything about this local event lined up. It was a situation that practically begged for student involvement with a relevant, compelling focus and the promise that some of the student writing might find its way to the newspaper. So she started off, assigning her students to study symptoms, treatments, preventions—whatever they could learn about cancer—and then to choose the type of writing they wanted to do, including informational pieces, interviews with survivors and caregivers, and personal stories. Students had to decide what genre might work best as a buildup for the event and what might play well with the community newspaper.

At this point, it sounds like a tidy package: a specific local context, one that students could grasp without too much difficulty. And it was pretty tidy. Editors at the paper embraced the idea of publishing student writing, especially since they picked the pieces. In this case, they wanted to feature a range of genres, which did not include pieces that simply listed what can be easily located online—for instance, "10 ways to avoid cancer." The student papers that made the cut went beyond merely reporting facts.

Hill's students discovered that if their writing was to be part of a community campaign, it had to be tailor-made and engaging enough to stir up interest and enthusiasm. They worked on new academic skills, including how to fold personal stories into their writing and how to select information that would have the most impact on their audience. Hill explains that her students' skills developed gradually, as did their understanding of the context, from a simple snapshot to something more complex:

> Most of my students started out writing very brief informational pieces. They would do short, facts-laden pieces describing different types of cancers, or about signs and symptoms. As time went on, students got better at blending genres and seemed to write more personal stories about people in our community who were battling cancer. They even became a little smarter about which informational topics would be interesting to the community—the opening of a caretaker hotel in Jackson or the history of Relay for Life, for example—rather than just spewing facts from WebMD. (All Hill quotes are from a personal communication, August 11, 2017.)

As it turned out, Hill kept the same students in her class from grades 8 through 10, so they had second and third chances to hit the mark. According to Hill, "The students became more sophisticated each year in their approaches, learning to think more about audience."

The community, too, learned something new. Hill explains: "For the first time, people in the community knew what was going on in the classroom and actually saw the students as members of the community. In fact, the project really blurred the lines between the school and the community."

STUDENT WRITING

Take a look at one of the published pieces by 9th-grader Hunter Blakeney (2014). Note the ways that this student's writing demonstrates his understanding of the context.

The Miracle of Living Beyond a Deadline
By Hunter Blakeney

My grandmother, Edith Parker, has stage 4 neuroendocrine pancreatic cancer. Even though she has cancer, I do not think of her illness when I think of who she is. I still see her as the same amazing woman she has always been. She is an extremely friendly person who can make anyone smile, and she is always there for her friends and family. She loves working in her garden, and I have many memories of hot summer days working alongside her in the flowerbeds.

Everything changed for my grandmother in July of 2010. Because she complained of stomach pain, my family took her to Wesley Medical Center in Hattiesburg. There, they did an MRI and found out that the stomach pains were anything but ordinary. They diagnosed her with cancer and told her that she did not have long to live, perhaps a year at most.

Every month for almost four years, my grandmother has gone to her oncology doctor and gotten a Sandostatin injection, a hormone that slows down the growth of cancer. Along with the shots, she receives a scan every four months to check the growth. Though not every visit has ended in good news, my grandmother continues to astound doctors time and again with her successful fight against what is usually a very aggressive type of cancer.

It would be safe to say that my grandmother is a miracle. She is still here today, four years later, even though her doctors said it would not be possible. In fact, her oncology doctor lost his own battle against cancer during this time, a reminder to her and to us that life can be unpredictable. She now likes to remind us: "Do not take anything for granted 'cause it can be gone in a snap."

My grandmother has inspired my family and me in so many ways. Even through all of the difficult times, she has not lost her ability to make others smile. I've seen her light up a hospital room and make her nurses cackle. And even though she doesn't get to do it as much as she'd like, Grandma still gets out in her yard to work. My grandmother has not allowed cancer to change who she is or keep her from doing what she enjoys. I love Grandma's determined spirit, and I am thankful to be her grandson.

Grandma has participated in Relay for Life for several years, and she plans on being there this year to support those who are fighting with her and to honor the memory of those who have lost the battle. Needless to say, I will be right by her side walking with her.

This year, I relay for Edith Parker—and for all of the men and women who are fighting to live beyond a deadline.

Please join us for the American Cancer Society's Relay for Life in Smith County on May 2nd in Raleigh, MS. It will be held on Main Street in Raleigh from 6:00 P.M. to 6:00 A.M. (p. 14)

Clearly, this student writer intends to rally community support for the Relay for Life event. He has chosen to motivate his audience to participate by telling an inspirational story with details about his grandmother and information about cancer treatment. His appeal is personal and emotional: His grandmother will walk and he will walk with her. "This year, I relay for Edith Parker—and for all of the men and women who are fighting to live beyond a deadline." The success of this piece of writing lies, in part, in the student's firm grasp of purpose, audience, and situation.

But there's also something else going on. In this case, the writer *connects* with the context. He cares about the subject of this piece and what the piece might accomplish. He wants to shine a light on his grandmother and where her cancer fits into his unwavering admiration of her.

It's easy to spot what we call Mojo on the sports field, when a player is fired up and making all the right moves. The same can be true for a highly motivated, emboldened writer. What's also true for the athlete and the writer is that when they make something happen for the fans or the audience, they can also make something happen for themselves. Their achievement has meaning and personal value.

MOJO BUILDER #2: HELPING WRITERS COME UP WITH CONTENT
#beefingupmojo

You may remember Jaime Escalante from the 1988 movie *Stand and Deliver*. He was a real-life teacher who gave his students the confidence and content knowledge to succeed. In the movie, his character takes on a group of dispirited students and turns them into geniuses, with the top scores on the Advanced Placement calculus test in the state. When the testing company challenges their success, the Escalante character goes to town again, convincing his Latino students that they can pop out the same scores twice when they are retested. The test within the test was whether the students could fire on all cylinders twice. Did they have the Mojo? (They did.)

In his book *Mojo: How to Get It, How to Keep It, How to Get It Back if You Lose It*, Marshall Goldsmith (2009) explains his idea of Mojo this way: "You're moving forward, making progress, achieving goals, clearing hurdles, passing the competition—and doing so with increasing ease. What you are doing matters and you enjoy doing it" (p. 5).

Each item in Goldsmith's list rings true. Of course, we want forward momentum for our student writers and some evidence that they are reaching new heights. The teacher in our next classroom closeup has some ideas about how to beef up her students' Mojo. As you read her story, think about how she immerses her students in research. They read articles, listen to experts, search for information online, and explore/observe firsthand, in person. This combination of research builds up their Mojo because they have something to say and a reason to say it.

CLASSROOM CLOSEUP: BUILDING AND SHAPING CONTENT
#reimagingingpurvis #investingincommunity

Brooke Ann McWilliams teaches middle school students in Purvis, Mississippi, a small farming town (population 2,322 in 2014). People don't flock to Purvis. In fact, they often leave for more opportunity. Businesses go elsewhere, too, abandoning the town and its buildings. It's no surprise, then, that students are not invested in the community and actually know little about it. McWilliams explains:

> I grew up in a small town myself. I already lived these students' lives. I watched people graduate and run off. I really didn't know much about my community, or even the idea of community. So I decided we had work to do. (Personal communication, August 11, 2017)

To start out, McWilliams and her students studied how Purvis came to be and how it has fared over the years. (In 1907, the town thrived with nine general stores, two newspapers, and a large sawmill. The very next year, a tornado wiped out the business district and Purvis stagnated.) Armed with information about their town, students branched out, reading about other communities in developing countries and the kinds of issues that crop up, from child labor to water shortages. McWilliams explains why this first foray into research was critical for her students:

> Many of them have rarely ventured out of our rural town, and several have only been as far as our neighboring city about 15 miles away. These students knew very little about dire global situations or other cultural lifestyles and what advocates/humanitarians are doing to help change the lives of others. Before I could ask them to go out and make our town a better place, I wanted to inform them and inspire them to enhance the quality of life for themselves and others. (All

McWilliams quotes in the remainder of this chapter are from a personal communication, January 1, 2018.)

Firsthand Research
#upcloseandpersonal

The idea that middle school students might choose some way to improve their community came to McWilliams as a way to promote civic pride and do some real good. At the same time, she wanted to get her students up and running in less familiar genres—specifically, informational writing and argument.

To focus their thinking after the readings, she challenged them to think of ways they could "make a difference locally." Using ideas from the articles, they came up with everything from planting community gardens to painting murals to encouraging healthy lifestyles.

At this point, McWilliams shepherded her classroom community into the community at large. As they looked around, she asked students to take on various roles: as a first-time visitor to the town; as a person who might not be able to use the park, library, and sidewalks the way kids can; and as a person who has lived in town most of his/her life and does not want to change the look/feel of the community.

> We walked for an hour, taking notes in our writers' notebooks and pictures with our cellphones. Really, the kids had no clue about so much of the town, like a museum no one visits anymore. The curator had to let us in. We talked to the clerk and judge at the courthouse where we had appointments. What made a lasting impression were the empty buildings, real eyesores. What could we put in those buildings, we wondered.

Back in the classroom, students pulled out their writers' notebooks, looked over their pictures, and studied a map of the town, brainstorming ideas for things they could propose that would make people want to live in Purvis. "They found things to enhance," McWilliams recalled. "They used my phone to start checking things out, to find people in town willing to help. They googled phone numbers and looked up websites on their Chromebooks, searching especially for ways to make money."

> The students came up with ideas to make people want to live in our community.
> —Brooke Ann McWilliams

For McWilliams, increasing students' Mojo meant giving them some specific strategies to help them bulk up content for their Humanitarian Projects, as she named them, and then work strategically and thoughtfully with that content, doing things like the following:

- Giving students a chance to see things on foot
- Offering students "new eyes" with which to see their town, through advance reading and by trying on different roles as they toured
- Emphasizing ownership of their community and their projects
- Asking students to take on reasonable, as opposed to intractable, problems
- Allowing students to choose the focus of their project, thereby increasing the chance that students might care more about their writing

Some Hallmarks of a Humanitarian Project
#makeitreal #definethemission

McWilliams required a mission statement for every proposed project. Students Elizabeth Puckett and Zella Holzinger found their mission on a neglected walking track:

Behind the Purvis Library, there is a walking track, but it isn't a safe place to walk. There are many holes in the ground and there is an old water fountain that no longer works. The walking track is also close to the road so it isn't safe for the people who walk there. We propose that we make the track safer, add in a water fountain, and make a nice place to sit if you need to rest while walking.

As mission statements go, this one has definite pluses. It crystalizes the problem (unsafe, dilapidated conditions) and gives reasons and suggestions for upgrading the track. It articulates a purpose and sets out a general scope of work. And it's real in the sense that real proposals and real organizations have mission statements with serious goals and intentions to make things happen. Like other legitimate proposals, students had to give an informed estimate of the cost and ideas for fundraising. In the case of the walking track, the students suggested making money by selling food, soliciting donations, and holding an auction.

Once the students had presented their projects to one another, some were bold enough to send their proposals to the mayor, who, in addition to his public job, also worked at the lumberyard. He managed to find time to come to the school auditorium to talk about what ideas were feasible and why. McWilliams explains the importance of this encounter with the mayor: "Students are used to fast solutions in this Google generation. But they need to learn that there are processes for making change."

McWilliams's students worked within a defined framework that did not require them to actually solve the problems they were investigating. Rather, the ultimate goal of the Humanitarian Project was for students to experience how citizens go about making change and to encourage future civic actions. In the process, they learned academic skills as they conducted research, organized content, and wrote proposals and mission statements, all of which contribute to Mojo.

Engaging a Wider Audience
#writingpublicly #socialvoice

No doubt interacting with leaders in the community was a new experience for McWilliams's students. Given the opportunity, they were able to test out their newfound authority through emails and personal contact. They learned to adapt their communication to people who could help, to make appeals, and to ask for information.

An essential experience for establishing authority, according to Stan Pesick, former teacher and district history–social studies coordinator, is engaging with a wider audience: "Students need to connect to a significant issue, have command of that issue, and figure out how to communicate it to the public" (all Pesick quotes in this chapter are from a personal communication, November 7, 2017).

In his proposal for improving Purvis, student Ramsey Walker writes this appeal for new playground equipment to accommodate children with disabilities. The writing demonstrates his understanding of a significant issue and his authority in communicating with a wider audience:

Do you know how it feels to go to the playground and enjoy yourself? Yes, many Americans know the feeling, but there are people who are handicapped and don't know the feeling. If we put a handicapped area in the park, they will have the freedom to enjoy a park as well as we do.

You might notice the public, social voice here, which is quite different from an academic, "in-school" voice. Young Whan Choi, former teacher and manager of performance assessments in the Oakland Unified School District, observes what changes for students when they are writing to an audience who is not the teacher: "They write with a different identity than just as a student. They write more from a place of agency and appeal, and less formulaically. They see themselves as having a voice that matters" (personal communication, January 4, 2018).

> All advocacy is, at its core, an exercise in empathy.
> —Samantha Power

The following email exchange illustrates the out-of-school voice Pesick and Choi find so important. You wouldn't necessarily know that student Andee Robertson's message comes from a 7th-grader. She assumes the identity of someone who is going to get things done. She makes a professional connection with an outside audience by linking a previous encounter to her current request. It's a we-are-in-this-together appeal that establishes a relationship and sets up the expectation of a positive response. Indeed, she gets a positive response, one that takes her request seriously and includes an open invitation to meet in person:

From: Andee Robertson
Sent: Friday, January 27, 2017 9:09 AM
To: Martin Hankins
Subject: Playground Grant

Thank you so much for speaking to us yesterday! We learned so much about our community and the justice system! I am writing to ask who I should contact if I want to add playground equipment at the park. I would love to make the park a more quality place to play and relax for ALL children and adults. If I get the go ahead I will begin the process of applying for the grant to receive the equipment. Thank you for any guidance you can give me.

P.S. I have also applied for a Little Free Library book box and if I receive a box I would like to set it up in the park and I would be the steward for it, too.

From: Martin Hankins
Date: Fri, Jan 27, 2017 1:04 PM
Subject: Playground Grant
To: Andee Robertson
Andee:

Thanks for your email. Enjoyed having the opportunity to speak with you and the others in the class. Please feel free to stop by anytime. I've copied Shelia Speights on our email as she is the clerk for the City of Purvis and can help you with any questions you may have regarding the playground equipment. She can share this information with the board of Aldermen and the Mayor as these are the people who make the decisions regarding the park. Let me know if we can help you with anything else.
Thanks,
Martin D. Hankins, LUTCF
Lamar County Circuit Clerk

In thinking ahead about this project, McWilliams envisioned that students would find value in their small community. According to Stan Pesick, "Every piece of public writing has a moral undertone. Values underline the way we see the world. One of the purposes of this kind of writing is to encourage discourse and caring about a subject. Students come to understand what's at stake and why."

In the Humanitarian Project that follows, take a look at the extent to which the student demonstrates a public, social voice, a moral stance, and an appeal to a wider audience.

Student Writing

Our Little Free Library
By Andee Robertson

Mission: A Little Free Library is a way to inspire young readers to reach for the stars and always chase their dreams. The Impact Fund they have created is a way for stewards who don't have the finances to provide one for the community.

My Dream for our Community: In our little community of Purvis, MS, we have always been joined together through sports, and just the fact that we are a small area. However, some of the kids in our town have never been able to come together and express their love of reading and learning, because they may not have access to books at home or their parents don't have time to stop by the public library and help the child get a library card. Although, the hope that we will be provided with one of these libraries is not only a sacred thing for the kids in this area but also for the parents who did not have a chance at being able to trade and discuss books with their friends growing up. I know myself and my community are hopeful and thrilled to maybe get the opportunity to come together and develop educational skills outside of the classroom.

Receival of my Library: To receive my library, I have applied for a grant\fund through the Little Free Library association that provides a free box with the commitment that I will be the steward for the library for at least a year which mandates me to add the library to their world map, keep it in good condition and fully stocked for at least a year, submit a picture with the library once it is installed, and finally hold at least one community gathering in the first year, which can include a book gathering for any age group.

Costs: Thanks to the Little Free Library's Program to help out communities and prepare the town's kids to become successful adults this project will cost nothing if we receive the grant. Besides the installing step which will mostly be done by volunteers.

My email to City Clerk, Sheila Speights:
My name is Andee Robertson and I am a 7th grader at Purvis Middle School. I was told by Mr. Martin Hankins to contact you about my ideas to better the park. As you may know, me and my class took a walking field trip around the town Wednesday to see ways we can better our community and the things I saw really opened my eyes to all the things that could be improved around town to help engage the younger generation. I would like for you to know that I have applied for a grant through the Little Free Library impact fund to receive one of their book boxes to educate younger and older readers. And if I am lucky enough to be granted this wonderful opportunity I would like to also place this in the park so that everyone may have access to it. I would be the steward of the library which means I will take care of the book box, replenish the amount of books, and also hold book gatherings for younger readers to attend. I will be so appreciative for any advice or suggestions you can give me.

Payoff for the Student
#morethanagrade

You may agree that this proposal/project report contains an earnest, moral tone, and certainly the writer has what Pesick calls "command of the issue." Opportunities to become an authority and to make an ardent plea happen infrequently in school. In this case, the student has also performed several beneficial civic actions by communicating with various public officials and by actually applying for a grant.

For those who argue that in the end, civic engagement projects are just another classroom exercise (after all, the report ultimately goes to the teacher for a grade), we offer an alternate view here. When it comes to making an impact, it's hard to beat the outcome of Andee Robertson's Humanitarian Project. Though she did not get her Little Free Library grant, she got something else, according to her mother, Lindsay Robertson:

> I was very blessed to see a dramatic change in my daughter with her being more aware of the world and community around her. She became more passionate about discovering needs in her community and actively pursuing ways she could contribute and create change. Authentic exposure paired with research and exploration lit a fire in my child that has forever changed her perception of her role in the world around her. (Personal communication, January 11, 2018)

Classroom Notes
#projectelements

A practical issue for McWilliams at the outset was communicating a set of requirements suitable for students of all ability levels. (Hers is an inclusion class with students ranging from special education to gifted.) Here is a list of the required elements that support project management and shift responsibility to the students, while at the same time leaving room for a range of responses:

1. Proposal Title
2. Brief Description of Your Project
3. Justification (Why are you proposing this? How will this benefit our community?)
4. Image
5. Cost
6. Contact (Who will you need to work with to make this happen?)
7. Grants/Applications/Fundraisers (How will you pay for your proposal?)

TEACHING PLAYBOOK
#nurturingmojo

The exercises in this playbook have several things in common. They invite students to identify what makes a piece of writing work. They are most effective when you use them more than once (think "sustainable"), and at some point, when you have students try out the exercises on their own writing. Most important, they are up for adoption and adaptation. You can take them for a little spin or give them some real traction with strategic repetition. We recommend traction.

Learning the Features of Good Writing
#applausemeter

EPIC
HOT
PRETTY HOT
WARM
COLD

Many teachers already use writing models—both student and professional—to illustrate features of a particular genre, of some specific writing skill or craft, of expectations or standards, and so on. What makes this exercise a little different is its generative nature:

1. Invite students to make judgments about the features of good writing or a certain kind of writing, using an applause meter. Like a rubric, the applause meter is open for teachers and students to create descriptors for each indicator. Rebekah Caplan, former teacher and codirector of the Bay Area Writing Project, who invented this exercise, uses these labels: *cold, warm, pretty hot, hot, epic.*
2. Show a writing model in parts, rather than as a whole, perhaps one paragraph at a time. Start by asking students about the features of the first part and where the first part falls on the meter. Then, add a paragraph or two and see what more unfolds in the writing and how it affects the meter. Keep adding and reassessing.
3. After a lot of practice with models, have students apply the meter to their own writing.

Test out the applause meter yourself on excerpts from the famous graduation speech George Saunders gave at Syracuse University on May 11, 2013 (as cited in Lovell, 2013). Stop after Part One and see if you can name some of the features that work well. Give it a spot on the meter. Then move to part two and see how this addition might change your ranking and think about why.

Part One:

Down through the ages, a traditional form has evolved for this type of speech, which is: Some old fart, his best years behind him, who, over the course of his life, has made a series of dreadful mistakes (that would be me), gives heartfelt advice to a group of shining, energetic young people, with all of their best years ahead of them (that would be you).

Now, one useful thing you can do with an old person, in addition to borrowing money from them, or asking them to do one of their old-time "dances," so you can watch, while laughing, is ask: "Looking back, what do you regret?" . . . So: What do I regret? Being poor from time to time? Not really. Working terrible jobs, like "knuckle-puller in a slaughterhouse?" . . . No. I don't regret that. Skinny-dipping in a river in Sumatra, a little buzzed, and looking up and seeing like 300 monkeys sitting on a pipeline, pooping down into the river. . . . Not so much.

Part Two:

But here's something I do regret: In seventh grade, this new kid joined our class. . . . Ellen was small, shy. She wore these blue cat's-eye glasses that, at the time, only old ladies wore. When nervous, which was pretty much always, she had a habit of taking a strand of hair into her mouth and chewing on it.

So she came to our school and our neighborhood, and was mostly ignored, occasionally teased ("Your hair taste good?"—that sort of thing). I could see this hurt her. (As cited in Lovell, 2013).

Even from these bits and pieces you get the idea of how the features build. In Part One, you probably picked out the engaging opening, the use of humor, the direct appeal to the audience, the effective listing of examples that build reader curiosity. (What will the speaker regret if not these experiences?)

Part Two begins a little story that illustrates what the speaker does regret. Anecdotes can bring the message home, and in this speech, the message is about kindness. What the speaker regrets most in his life are failures of kindness.

Some last thoughts about the applause meter. As with most catchy, engaging ideas, this one can easily become a gimmick, rather than a serious look at what counts in writing and at what could be better. What makes a piece epic? The learning is in the ongoing search. In fact, for students to gain enough confidence, authority, and Mojo to pick out what works in a piece of writing, they need plenty of practice over time.

Analyzing Photos as a Way to Talk About Writing
#3minuteessays

Our colleague Rebekah Caplan invented this exercise for a recent group of high school students in Kuwait as a way to bolster their confidence and ability to pinpoint what makes writing effective.

Start by showing students some photos that grab attention or provoke a reaction. Ask them the following questions, each to be answered in a 3-minute essay:

1. Why do people like photos?
2. Which one of these photos draws you in and why?
3. What's happening in the photo you chose? Tell the story.
4. The photographer probably took this photo because . . .

Students present their choices and responses in small groups. Making and defending critical judgments is one direct route to getting your Mojo. Applying those critical judgments to a particular piece of writing is the next step—for example, why do people like stories? Which one of these stories draws you in? And so on.

Having Something to Say
#Iremember #Iknow

The following exercise is a classic—so much a part of the drinking water in the writing world that you can find variations all over the Internet. Here, we provide an example of the classic version, followed by an adaptation useful in the disciplines for coming up with content.

1. *Generating memories.* Ask students to make a list of 10 things they remember from their life experiences. Each sentence in the list begins with the words, "I remember": for example, "I remember the time I set the oven on fire" or "I remember when I released the parking brake and sent the car down the hill."
2. *Generating more memories and possibilities beyond the initial list.* Have students select one "I remember" to share with the class or in a small group. They will hear memories that will remind them of others they haven't thought of in their own lives. As they listen to one another, invite them to jot down any memory that has possibilities for them.
3. *Going deeper.* Ask students to select one of their "I remembers" as a potential topic for their writing and to write a paragraph about why this memory stands out for them. Taking young writers beyond the concrete experience to more abstract thinking adds an important dimension. By reflecting on their experience, they can come up with its significance, with key details, and with a reason for writing about it—not to mention an almost ready-made conclusion to their piece.

These steps may appear fixed and finite. But that's an illusion! What counts here is the idea of activating what kids know and, for that matter, teaching them they really do have something to say.

Students also have bona fide disciplinary knowledge that is worth sharing with their classmates before the informative lecture or before they turn to their computers. For example, in a social studies or science class, students can first draw on what's inside their heads. The process looks somewhat the same as the one above. Students make a list beginning their sentences with "I know," and then share an item on their list, generating together an initial body of knowledge. They can also share their questions about a topic—another way to bring to the surface what they already know and would like to know next. As an alternative to simply handing over the content or the resources to find the content, this exercise gives students the message that they are capable, competent, and ready to learn more—a message that boosts Mojo.

> When authors write about the people and places they know, or the things they do, we hear a truth.
> —Rich Kent

Final Thoughts About Mojo
#feelthepower

Teachers like Hayley Hill help students connect intellectually and emotionally with their writing context. Brooke Ann McWilliams builds experiences for her students that arm them with content and authority. Along the way, students in both classes also learn new skills (a key Mojo builder): conducting research, blending genres, using personal stories, writing mission statements, making arguments, trying out a public voice. These strategies have a big payoff. As Goldsmith (2009) reminds us, Mojo is the moment when we do something that's purposeful, powerful, and positive.

In writing and in life.

CHAPTER 3

Writing Your Narrative

Being able to tell a good story has social value. People want to know about other people. Many of us are shameless voyeurs when it comes to Facebook, Instagram, Snapchat, and the like. We hang out on social media for photos of our friends' or celebrities' lives, their children, their pets, their lunches and dinners. We often talk about each other in storybook terms: "That's her narrative" or "Now he's spinning a new narrative."

From the point of view of the storyteller, a narrative becomes

> a form of identity, in which the things someone chooses to include in the story, and the way she tells it can both reflect and shape who she is. A life story doesn't just say what happened, it says why it was important, what it means for who the person is, for who they'll become, and for what happens next. (Beck, 2015, para. 5)

In other words, we all have a narrative floating around in our heads. Even small children know how to tell a story, although some of them might drag on and on. Tom Newkirk (2014) reminds us, "We have literary minds that respond to plot, character, and details in all kinds of writing.... [A]s humans, as time-bound mortals, we must tell stories" (p. 146).

However, narrative writing has a way of disappearing in school. The thinking seems to be that it's fine for 1st-graders, but once students are over 3 feet tall, they no longer need chances to tell their stories. Somehow narratives get the boot early in the school game, considered too "soft" to be in the running for a hardcore academic curriculum with its emphasis on the "real" stuff like persuasion and argument. Teacher and author Linda Christensen (2009) mocks this traditional trajectory of the writing curriculum:

> In telling the story of how you became who you are, and of who you're on your way to becoming, the story itself becomes a part of who you are.
> —Julie Beck

> Students learn to write narratives in elementary school; in high school, they need to move up to essays. The genre-apartheid approach to teaching writing is

wrong-headed for many reasons.... The division between narrative and essay is fluid. Most great essayists, like George Orwell, Joan Didion, Henry Louis Gates, bell hooks, and Annie Dillard, employ narrative strategies in their work. (pp. 60–61)

In fact, stories rule our lives. They are part of all the reading, writing, and viewing we do. As Donald Murray (2013) points out, narrative is "embedded in all effective writing," including:

the proposal for a new marketing plan, the essay on health care, the insurance investigator's report, the sermon, the scholarship application, the restraining order, the memorial service remarks. All are built on the sturdy and time-tested foundation of narrative. (pp. 89–90)

We are squarely in the camp that believes good writing, *writing to make an impact*, includes storytelling. What counts as "academic" writing in school often cries out for an anecdote, a reminiscence, or an illustrating event. According to Mayher, Lester, and Pradl (1983), stories are "the jumping off point—the way in" to argument (p. 13). Tom Newkirk (2014) calls narrative our "home base" in writing: "It [narrative] is there to ground abstract ideas, to help us see the pattern in a set of numerical data, to illuminate the human consequences of political action. It is home base" (p. 5).

In other words, our narratives are our workhorses. They make something happen for us and for our audiences.

ABOUT THIS CHAPTER: DOING JUSTICE TO NARRATIVE

We offer two classroom closeups from two Mississippi teachers. The first shows how narrative functions as the "jumping-off place" for all kinds of writing. Emma Richardson encourages and teaches her students to use personal stories as part of their college application essays—stories that become the launching pad for candidates to show their character, goals, challenges, and accomplishments.

In the second closeup, Bill Kirby pulls no punches with his students as he tries to deprogram them from their reliance on formulas and other crutches that too often go along with school writing. In Kirby's view, for a narrative to make an impact, it has to be meaningful to the student and, at the same time, it has to be worth reading for an audience. We end the chapter with ideas in the teaching playbook and resources that complement Richardson's and Kirby's approaches.

> Narratives provide one of the few opportunities for students to write or talk about their lives in school.
> —Linda Christensen

CLASSROOM CLOSEUP: LETTING STORIES DO THE WORK
#captivatingreaders #thepizzazfactor

Journey Through the Rain
By Rachel Jones

Raindrops in Mississippi are always fat. They fall from clouds no longer able to hold them and slide through the humidity, making a murky storm soup suspended in the atmosphere. In an early memory, I am standing outside the Boys and Girls Club peering into the soupy haze of this particular storm, waiting for my mother. Our routine is to walk, often hand in hand, through the "old projects" to our home in the "new projects." Will we walk today? In a soft, rattled voice, I tell Mr. Tony, the counselor, that she'll be here soon— and she is. Dainty, and cowering beneath the barrage of wind and rain, she stands behind a tree, pulls her flimsy hood tighter over her face and flicks her wrist, beckoning me to come forward.

My mother feels it is her duty to teach me everything: how to long divide, how to play defense on the soccer field, how to follow through with my backhand, how to control my breathing when I run, how to protect myself, how to make one night's meal last a week. She force feeds me each lesson with the firmness and sass I'm sure only a Southern woman can. But I ate my most valuable lesson when I saw her standing in the rain, soggy and focused: No matter the severity of the storm, if you have somewhere to go, you will just have to walk. . . . (Quoted in Fallows, 2014)

This excerpt from a Mississippi high school senior in Emma Richardson's creative writing class did not fall from the clouds, nor is it the writing of a one-of-a-kind brilliant student, although we certainly recognize its brilliance. Rather, this piece illustrates specific strategies students learn from Richardson and also from their classmates, such as effective openings, developing a topic by telling a story, using sensory details evoking people or places, establishing point of view and tone, and selecting active verbs and figurative language. In our opinion, it also qualifies as *writing to make an impact* because it transports the reader into a visual soup of fat raindrops and then to the moment of truth when the narrator's mother shows up, despite the storm. Richardson agrees that this kind of writing "enables the reader to *learn to see*":

It offers a way of *seeing*, a way to stretch the reader's (or viewer's) *vision*, a way for humans to break out of the prisons of their own skins and to see things from someone else's perspective. (All Richardson quotes are from a personal communication, September 17, 2017.)

Richardson points out another reason to put this writing in the category of making an impact: "Poetic writing helps students bring shape and form to their experience. They come to a sense of clarity about who they are and they find out what they know."

The little story above about rain and a mother who gives her child a life lesson by showing up in that rain led into a college entrance essay. Take a look at two more paragraphs as the story moves along:

The little storms of life have left me doused. The wind of my parents' perennial unemployment has blown away my umbrella. The chill of watching my mother scrape together dollar bills and dirty quarters to pay rent and wash our clothes has frozen me to the bone. The endless drizzle of watching my mother scrape alone, as the convicted felon I call "father" keeps his distance, has soaked through my raincoat.

Despite the rain, I have a destination that I'm determined to reach. My destination is having a thorough understanding of calculus. It's having a killer serve. It's running a marathon. It's executing a flawless bicycle kick. It's writing a set of words that thousands of people will digest and want more of. It's looking into someone's eyes and knowing I've helped. My destination is excellence. (Quoted in Fallows, 2014)

One thing is clear in this stormy weather piece with its extended metaphor: The student has deftly used an everyday story to lead into snapshots of challenging experiences in her past and ambitions for her future. The piece contains what Andrew B. Cohen (1990) refers to as the "pizazz factor." In his article "Write Us an Essay, Buster, and Make It Interesting—or Else," Cohen notes that "Nearly all college admissions officials will admit that, left to themselves, most high-school seniors will submit essays of stupefying dullness.... Admissions people want to have fun, too" (p. A1). Cohen cites one essay question posed many years ago by the Massachusetts Institute of Technology that invited students to "feel free to use your imagination, recognizing that those who read it [your essay] will not mind being entertained" (p. A1).

Richardson borrowed the phrase "pizazz factor" for her unpublished monograph *The Pizazz Factor: Writing Successful College-Application Essays* (2014), in which she emphasizes the need for storytelling and poetic prose. Here, she lists some elements of poetic prose (see Figure 3.1) that make college application essays more "interesting—or else."

Richardson gives narratives cachet, positioning them as central to high-stakes writing, rather than something to be checked off in elementary school. The fact that narrative can make something happen in real-life arguments, such as applications, sales pitches, campaigns, and editorials, as well as in all academic subjects, is reason enough to resurrect it wherever it might be missing in the curriculum. Notice all the opportunities for storytelling in Richardson's suggested practice prompts for college application essays in Figure 3.2.

Figure 3.1. Elements of Poetic Prose

a. Using active verbs instead of linking verbs
b. Eliminating "empty" adjectives (especially "labels," such as *interesting, cute, nice, great, pretty, sweet, gross, ugly* ...)
c. Eliminating adverbs (especially "intensifiers" or "qualifiers," such as *very/really* and *rather/fairly*)
d. Using participles
e. Using sensory images
f. Using figurative language
g. Using dialogue
h. Achieving specificity or "chunkiness"; using items-in-a-series

Figure 3.2. Additional Prompts for College Application Essays

☺ What person has influenced you the most? Probably the appearance of that person is not as important as his/her words and actions, but your reader would like to be able to picture that person in his mind.

   You can probably hear that person's voice in your head even as you're reading this. What are some of the sayings of that person? Let your reader hear them. When you often talked with that person, where were you? In a car? a truck? a deer stand? a kitchen? a store? a porch? Let your reader see the place.

   Why is that person important in your life? How will that person continue to influence you throughout your life? Feel free to write in a lighthearted tone; your reader won't mind being entertained! Sometimes the people who are most memorable and influential to us are those who make us laugh.

☺ What is your *passion*? What do you do when you *don't have to do anything*? What activity fills you with *joy*? Is it when you read? Play the piano? Play the guitar? Watch movies? Work calculus problems? Write? Take photographs?

   When did your passion begin? When did you realize you had become passionate about that activity? What does your passion for that activity say about you?

☺ "I've Got a Secret": Do you have a special *gift* for doing something other people have difficulty with or just don't like to do? For example, do you enjoy reading instruction manuals for cell phones or digital cameras? Are you the only one in your family who can re-fold a highway map? Have you actually always enjoyed being in the kitchen/on the porch at family reunions listening to family stories instead of being in the den watching the football game on television?

   What does that "secret" or "gift" reveal about you? How does it make you a good candidate for college admission or for the lucrative scholarship?

☺ Did you immigrate to the United States from somewhere far away? Or did your parents immigrate to the U.S. a few years before you were born? Have you "juggled" two cultures and two languages almost all your life?

   How has that shaped your life and your perspective? Why is that important for a college admissions committee to know about you? Will it help you "navigate" the "new culture" of a college or university? (Richardson, 2014, pp. 5–6)

In the next classroom closeup, narrative flourishes with all its possibilities for linking life experiences with writing in school. But first, Bill Kirby's students have to unlearn some of the school writing formulas they have relied on in the past. Unlearning something requires a full-court press. Ever try turning down chocolate when the candy box is open and under your nose?

CLASSROOM CLOSEUP: MAKING NARRATIVE SING
#formulafreezone

Bill Kirby came to teaching in his mid-30s but found himself floundering in a school with a lock-step, formulaic English curriculum. At the time, he thought, "This is not the deal. I cannot see myself doing this." (Unless otherwise noted, all Kirby quotes in this chapter are from a personal communication, July 26, 2017.) Twenty-nine years later, Kirby is still teaching, now in Petal, Mississippi.

No surprise, Kirby looks for alternatives to what he views as strictly school writing. He begins by describing to his students what he hopes never to see— "fluff"—"vague papers that don't say a thing." He shows his class examples of "fluff" paragraphs and contrasts those with writing that is carefully considered and purposeful. "Being deliberate," he tells his students, "is so much more fun and powerful than fluff."

What Is "Fluff?"
#thestuffinfluff

Every teacher who lives and breathes has examples of "fluff." No matter how many hours you spend teaching students to give examples and details, no matter how often you respond to papers with the admonition "be specific," no matter how many times you gnash your teeth, it's inevitable. Students somehow come equipped with a gift for fluff. But just to be sure we are talking about the same stuff in fluff, read through the paragraph below, paraphrased from a student application essay to an esteemed university. You'll recognize the pattern of generalities, we guarantee it:

I know that this University is the right university for me. Journalism is my passion and I know I will be able to be a great success in my field with an excellent education.

Academically speaking, there is no equal to the School of Journalism. This is the place for me to expand my horizons. It allows me to learn how to better my reporting skills. In this setting, the possibilities are endless. My time at your school is going to change my life.

The University and the School of Journalism are my passion and I hope to meet the faculty and other students to show them that this is where I belong.

So earnest and eager. Such a likable candidate. But what do we really know about the writer, his qualifications and character? This piece illustrates some of the well-known features of fluffy writing, writing that does the following:

- Relies on general statements, one after the other
- Provides limited or no examples, evidence, anecdotes, specific details, images, names, places
- Uses some kind of predetermined formula into which the content is inserted, regardless of the nature of the content
- Repeats words, phrases, and ideas, usually for lack of something to say
- Lacks a purposeful sequencing of ideas or events
- Lacks organic transitions in favor of *then*, *next*, or *the first reason*, *the second reason*
- Routinely repeats, restates, summarizes, or recaps in the conclusion
- Lacks impact

Read on for ideas for transforming fluff.

Offering Choices
#whatsyourstory?

To start with, students in Kirby's class use stories from their lives, material that is close at hand. They have some attachment to the content because they've lived it. They have access to examples and details. What's more, their stories are a way of connecting to other human beings and making their voices heard. They also decide on exactly which story they will write about—a seemingly simple practice with gold medal potential.

Giving students choices positively affects learning, according to Paula Denton (2005), who examined 32 studies focused on the payoffs of providing choice in grades K–12:

> Most of the research demonstrated that when students had choices in their learning, they became highly engaged and productive. They were excited about learning and shared their knowledge. They were likely to think more deeply and creatively, work with more persistence, and willingly use a range of academic skills and strategies. (p. 2)

Kirby also claims that when students make choices, they are more likely to value what they are writing about. He is not alone in promoting personal meaning as a cornerstone. "If the writing project has no meaning or the student has only a small stake in what they are writing about or why they are writing about it they won't really care or take it seriously" (Eodice, Geller, & Lerner, 2017, p. 1).

Kirby talks with his students about the decisions they need to make when they choose their topics:

This is your chance to write about what you want to write about. Be yourself. Don't use profanity or sex or violence or anything else edgy just to shock your reader. Write about whatever's important, funny, puzzling, or frustrating to you. You don't need anything magnificent or glorious. Your clarity and trueness will make your story worth hearing. (Personal communication, December 21, 2017)

We looked at three sets of papers from Kirby's classes to see what kinds of things his students wrote about when they had the freedom to choose topics that matter to them. These topics shout personal meaning:

- Challenges (living with disease or disability, dealing with families, losing a first love, moving to a new school)
- Disasters (family death, near-drowning, tornados, fire, not making the basketball team)
- Passions (drumming, baseball, skateboarding, piano)
- Obsessions (tests and grades)
- Getting in trouble

Studying Models
#Inrealtime #unpolished

Many teachers offer models of whatever they are asking students to do—models written by former students, professional pieces, favorite mentor texts, and so on. In the report *Writing Next*, Graham and Perin (2007) cite the study of models as one of the most effective practices for improving student writing because it "provides students with opportunities to read, analyze and emulate models of good writing" (p. 5). Yet as powerful as models seem to be, they might be even more effective when they are constructed in real time.

Years ago, we attended a rehearsal of California's Oakland Symphony to catch a glimpse of Calvin Simmons, who was, at the age of 28, the youngest African American conductor of a major orchestra. Simmons was on his meteoric way to fame, so we had high expectations, but no idea exactly what we would see. To our surprise, Simmons turned out to be a gifted teacher. At 6 foot 1, he towered over the musicians, no doubt giving him a panoramic view. Whether or not his height also gave him an advantage when it came to hearing every note, we couldn't tell you. But he frequently stopped the music to critique and ask for revisions in tempo or timing or whatever he felt needed shape or emphasis. It was a teaching session for everyone in the concert hall. Simmons swung around on occasion, commenting irreverently on things like the acoustics, which had to be accommodated somehow. This was the real deal—the drafting of a musical performance.

While models of finished pieces of writing give students options, expectations, and techniques, showing students a polished product may not always beat a real-time demonstration of how a piece of writing emerges seemingly out of thin air. Proponent Kelly Gallagher (2006) sees it this way:

> When I brought in my model essay for my students, I was doing nothing more than showing them the Grecian Urn. However, I had hidden from them the most valuable part—the steps, often torturous, I took to get to the polished product.
>
> When I assign a complex writing task now, I write alongside my students. While I write, I project my work on a screen for all to see. . . . I think out loud as I begin composing and ask my students to chart the number of decisions I make while writing my first paragraph. (pp. 52–53)

This kind of step-by-step is what we witnessed when we had our evening with Calvin Simmons. We watched a performance in the making with stops and starts and with reruns and on-the-spot revisions. We witnessed a critical component we would not have noticed had we only seen the finished performance—the conductor's decisions (not to mention his humor and his way of approaching what needs changing).

Like Simmons and Gallagher, Bill Kirby takes a workshop approach to writing, demonstrating his process for his students. He composes in real time and talks about what he is doing so students can observe his deliberations and decisions, and at the same time become more conscious of their own processes as they discover new ones. They watch him add and delete as he tries out different words and phrases:

> Students see that I experiment and make conscious choices as I write, and I'm not checking a rubric or scale. They also learn that you can write something badly and you don't have to throw yourself in front of a truck. You can change it.

Kirby depends on this kind of interaction with his students—the kind of back-and-forth that takes teachers out of the judge and jury role and instead creates a classroom of composers.

Classroom Talk About What Works
#openforum

At various times, Kirby and his students roam the room, looking at drafts posted on walls, listening to pieces read aloud, critiquing as they go, sometimes asking one another, "But what does it say?" They talk about possibilities, and they aren't afraid to laugh at themselves as they learn together what works and what doesn't. Kirby describes the transformation:

> For kids, the veil is lifted. For too many years, students and teachers have been victimized by publishers' commercial programs and state rubrics. Teachers have been afraid that kids would fall off the planet if they didn't have a formula, and kids love formulas because they can just plug everything in. Now, kids see that writing doesn't have to be BS, that they have some control.

The student-owned writing from Kirby's class also circulates on Google Docs and in the school hallways. With Kirby's encouragement, many students fly even higher, submitting their pieces to Scholastic or to Mississippi Rural Voices Radio. In doing so, they take yet another risk, putting their writing through a competitive process.

The ultimate prize, according to Kirby, is this: Kids finally see what it means to be a writer. "It's about making decisions, right down to choosing the right words in order to make things clear to another human being." Kirby tells his students, "That's what we do in life. I want you to carry this lesson with you every day, every moment you have an exchange in words with someone."

Teaching Craft
#bustingupfluff

Life in Kirby's class includes a series of short lessons on techniques that will bump up the quality of their writing—for example, how to include specific details, when repetition is effective, why and how to vary sentences. "I use the same exercises with struggling classes as I do in AP," Kirby says. "Their writing gets so much better and *they can see the difference*. They have some tools to make things coherent and meaningful" (italics added).

When writers can actually see what adding certain features like dialogue or specific details does for their writing, they can intentionally use those features again and again to create an effect on the reader. Especially for students who find learning to write an uphill battle filled with mystery, learning something tangible and visible provides some much-needed instant gratification. Note here that many of the narrative techniques Kirby and Richardson teach—eye-catching openings, deliberate word choices, powerful images—are appropriate in any kind of writing. See the teaching playbook for more examples of writing exercises that focus on visible improvements.

In the student writing excerpts that follow, look for evidence of Kirby's lessons and think about how the lessons might have catapulted students past "fluff."

Student Writing

In this opening paragraph about her first day in a new school in Mississippi, 11th-grader Kami Moler re-creates the tension of making her way alone through the building and into a classroom of students who see her as a stranger:

My dad dropped me off at my new school and I was greeted by sharp looks and dissatisfied faces. I walked into the guidance office, as advised, and instantly heard the sound of southern slang and elongated vowels. Since I'm from New Jersey, this was a new sound for me—I didn't like it. As I made my way through the hallways of doom, stepping on hot rocks, and dodging demons, I began to become even more flustered. My hands were shaking like maracas and sweat was slowly trembling down my skin, dampening the bottom back of my white shirt. I walked into my second block class and was greeted, again, by sharp looks but mixed with confusion. The teacher, Miss Chapman, introduced me to the class and told them how I was from the northeast. In that moment, everyone in the classroom looked at me like I was an extraterrestrial. When I sat down, light, southern accents drowned me in questions and false statements. "What's it like in New Jersey?" "I heard they're rude up there." "Why'd you move here?" The ocean was coming again—I tried to not let my anxiety get the best of me. I answered with a simple "nice", "they aren't", and "my dad's job". By fifth period I was labeled as "the new girl" and was brought up in various conversations by a few whispering strangers.

This excerpt shows evidence of Kirby's lessons on elaborated details and deliberate word choice. The writer walks us through her ordeal, using visual images (*my skin dampening the bottom back of my white shirt*), snippets of dialogue, and "show not tell" phrases (*southern accents drowned me in questions*). The scene captures the agony of being labeled as different.

> Always be a poet, even in prose.
> —Charles Baudelaire

In the next excerpt, from a piece entitled "Airport," Malcolm Collett writes about the final farewell moments as his brother leaves for the Navy—someone he has scrapped with his entire life and failed to appreciate:

Only Fifty feet away from the point of no return, we came to a halt. So many questions were rushing through my mind. 'What do I say? Why, why would

you do this to me?' But the most prominent was 'I'm gonna miss you bro.'
That's when he turned to me and gave me a hug! The only time we ever
made contact was when we fought. I felt like crying, but I can't show him my
feelings get to me. He says to me, "Be sure to take care of mom and dad. I'm
gonna miss you little bro." Then he spun and began walking towards his exit.
"Wait!" I shouted and began to bolt to him who pivoted 180 degrees in time
to catch me as I threw myself into his arms. Standing there silent, motionless,
holding one another, just brothers sad to lose the other. Slowly he let go,
giving one last look, and left for the exit.

Though perhaps a bit rough in spots, this concluding paragraph illustrates
exactly what Kirby is after. It's real. It's truthful. It shows the power and complexity of a relationship between brothers. By re-creating a pivotal moment,
the writer invites his audience to share his emotional breakthrough. Once
again, dialogue and specific visual details (*spun and began walking*; *pivoted 180
degrees*; *giving one last look*) create the emotional whammy.

The next selection comes from a much longer piece written by Deven Gill entitled "Opus 22," about a young boy who takes piano lessons from his demanding, often scolding grandmother. He continually disappoints her.

I butcher the piece. It is well out of my ability to play. The pages are marked
with many virtuosic runs and leaps. The sight of the notes on those pages
still baffle me. My mind attempts to run through the piece separate from my
hands, but even those hands which I imagine get tangled, twisted, left overall
confounded by the complexity of the music. The music is a disastrous and
chaotic failed attempt at beauty. When I finish, my grandmother doesn't carp,
and she doesn't reprimand; she sits there and says nothing in disbelief as I
remove my hands from the keys.

Once again, what stands out for us in this excerpt is the background music—Bill Kirby's lessons on exact word choice, effective repetition (*my grandmother doesn't carp, and she doesn't reprimand . . .*) and attention to sentence
variety, including a short sentence for dramatic emphasis (*I butcher the piece.*).
Recall that Kirby teaches students these particular strategies so they have a
toolkit to give their writing meaning and credibility.

For this last example, we selected two paragraphs from a piece entitled "Why I Run" by Landon Draughn—one from the middle of the piece and one from the end. You might note that the paragraphs represent two different time periods in the writer's life, tied together by the theme "never give up."

All my life I had been running. I ran for fun, ran for sports, and I even ran from my problems, but there was something about sprinting down a trail as fast as you can, trying to beat the best of the best that just always got me going. I was introduced to running at the age of 11, when my cousin, Caden, decided that he was going to try to get healthier and lose some weight. While that sounds all nice, what you don't know is that as a small child Caden was diagnosed with Leukemia and was only given months to live. I was too young to understand at the time so my parents just explained to me that I needed to spend as much time with him as possible. With all that being said, here I was 6 years later, running down my childhood street, trying to keep up with a kid that has cancer. Later that summer Caden passed unexpectedly, it was a day I'll never forget. One day he passed out in his living room and just never woke up; they said it was complications from his previous surgery. There I was, an 11 year old boy, with nothing left of him but the memories of our runs together, and the words that he told me that applied to so much more than just running. "Never give up." . . .

As the gun sounded, seven runners from the twenty five best schools in the state all charged forward, trying to get the best position at the front of the race. It's something that's hard to describe if you've never seen it, but it's almost like 200 wildebeest are running as fast as possible from a lion, and only the first survives. The sense of urgency in the group is shown through the heavy breathing, stomping of feet, and the occasional flying elbow. The race carried into the second mile where we once again passed the crowd. The scream of the fans seemed like something you would find at a college football game, not a high school cross country meet. After you passed the crowd, we entered the third mile of the race. The third mile of the race is by far the hardest mile of the race. Your adrenaline from the beginning of the race has now worn off, there are no crowds to cheer you on, and you have two other miles weighing your legs down. This is the part of the race where all the training and practice goes out the window, and it all comes down to who has the most heart. It comes down to who has the most to run for. It truly comes down to who wants it most. So as I made my way towards that finish line on that chilly Thursday morning, I decided I had the most to run for as those three words popped into my head. I saw Caden's face, as I started my sprint up the hill, to a third place finish in the race, and a memory that I will not soon forget.

What impressed us about this writing is its clear intention to make events vivid and understandable to an audience. Recall for a minute that Kirby posts student writing on the walls of his classroom so that everyone can talk about what works and how to improve what might not work as well. This practice puts the idea of audience front and center, and it shows up in the students' writing.

In the first paragraph, the writer gives the reader key moments in his early life—moments that set the stage for his dramatization of a cross-country race. Then, rather than delivering a blow-by-blow of a sporting event, the writer re-creates for his audience the trajectory of the race: the sights and sounds (*heavy breathing, stomping of feet, and the occasional flying elbow*) and the physical and mental drain on the runner (*Your adrenaline from the beginning of the race has now worn off, there are no crowds to cheer you on . . .*). Bringing a reader into the scene is often hard to pull off, especially in a piece that covers so much time and distance, both in years and in emotions.

TEACHING PLAYBOOK

Most experienced writers know how to engage their readers from the get-go. They aren't limited by too many rules. Nor do they need a special license to stretch the boundaries in order to attract an audience. However, for students to make the leap from a prescribed opening or from one that staggers around looking for a clear direction, they will likely benefit from concrete examples. Here are some we have used, along with links to many more. You can read and talk about these in class, or better yet, select model openings in local newspapers or in whatever you are reading in class. What does the author do to get the reader's attention? What makes these leads compelling?

Strategies for Compelling Openings
#startwithmodels

😊 *Using physical description:*
Murray Barr was a bear of a man, an ex-marine, six feet tall and heavyset, and when he fell down—which he did nearly every day—it could take two or three grown men to pick him up. (Gladwell, 2006, p. 96)

😊 *Providing a dramatic preview:*
Kelly Orgeron, wife of fiery LSU coach Ed Orgeron, had a medical emergency last summer that threatened her life. But her story and the obstacles she's faced and overcome go far beyond that. (Dellenger, 2018)

😊 *Piquing curiosity (typical approach to a sports lead):*
Cal's secondary has been driving opponents batty all season. On Saturday, they made the Washington coaching staff briefly blow a gasket. (Simmons, 2018, p. 1)

😊 *Dropping into the action:*
It was a wrong number that started it, the telephone ringing three times in the dead of night, and the voice on the other end asking for someone he was not. (Auster, 1994, p. 1)

😊 *First-person lead:*
I spent my final year in college worrying about the future. I would have a BA, with honors in sociology, prepared for absolutely nothing. (Reichl, 1998, p. 149)

😊 *A hook in science writing* (great openings are not limited to newspapers and fiction):
Maize is self-fertilized and wind-pollinated, botanical terms that don't begin to describe the beauty and wonder of corn sex. (Pollan, 2007, p. 28)

😊 *Scene setting:*
We arrived in Grand Rapids with five dollars and a knapsack of clothes. (Nguyen, 2007, p. 1)

😊 *Provocative first lines:*
Not every thirteen-year-old girl is accused of murder, brought to trial, and found guilty. (Avi, 1990, p. 1)

Other Resources for Good Leads

http://americanbookreview.org/100BestLines.asp
https://training.npr.org/digital/leads-are-hard-heres-how-to-write-a-good-one/
http://blogs.publishersweekly.com/blogs/shelftalker/?p=3550

An Exercise in Inventing New Leads
#starters #bedaring

In this exercise, students rewrite the openings below, trying out each strategy with a new sentence of their own:

- *Start with a question:* Do you write well enough to become a police officer? (Adapted from Kelly Gallagher, 2011)
- *Start with a quotation:* "I'm sick of running into potholes," my friend announced the other day. "This street looks like the face of the moon."
- *Start with a closeup and lots of sensory details:* "I am sitting at a kitchen table, a mid-century dinette set, looking down at a pile of gelatinous pasta topped with fried balls of Spam and ketchup." (Donoff, 2010, p. 13)
- *Start with a location:* "January 2003. Yukon. Whitehorse International Airport. The temperature is five to six below zero." (Brenna, 2010, p. 49)
- *Start with a provocative sentence:* "Lee was just six the first time she stole something." (Rose, 2017, p. 7)

Writing Satisfying Conclusions
#reflecting #dramatizing

Take another look at how Richardson's student Rachel Jones brought home the point of her story about her mother's journey in the rain (see p. 32). She doesn't use tired old signal phrases such as "in conclusion." She doesn't summarize what she has already written. She doesn't simply restate a thesis. Instead, sticking with her extended metaphor "the little storms of life," she explains in her closing what her journey has meant to her and "despite the rain" what goals she hopes to reach.

Not all young writers are adept at writing conclusions and may need help in reflecting on their experience or dramatizing its impact. The sentence starters below serve as prompts for students to bring home a story's significance.

The starters also lend themselves to brainstorming ways to conclude. Try looking at one student's draft together as a class and tossing out ideas for possible conclusions, using one or two sentence starters. Students can also work in pairs or small groups to help one another decide on the "so what" at the end of a piece.

Sentence Starters for Reflective Conclusions

- Looking back, I realize that ...
- One lesson I've learned is ...
- This experience taught me ...
- While at one time I thought ... now I ...
- After that day, I ...
- This action reveals ...
- The story reminds us ...

The idea here is to kick off some reflective thinking. If you are not a fan of sentence starters—which arguably can be a somewhat limited tool—consider turning some of the starters above into questions:

- What have you learned from your experience?
- Why did you make particular decisions or choices or judgments?
- Looking back, what would you have done differently?

Strategies for Writing with Specifics
#shownottell

Both Richardson and Kirby make a point of teaching students to transform generalities into specifics. Richardson refers to using sensory details, while

Kirby thinks in terms of selective and deliberate word choice. In either case, the idea is to help students "show, not tell."

In her book *Writers in Training*, Rebekah Caplan (1984) suggests using short daily workouts that focus on "show not tell" as a way to teach students alternatives to writing with vague generalities. Caplan assigns her students a telling sentence each day. They return to class the following day with a showing paragraph. Caplan selects several of the paragraphs on the spot to read aloud and critique with the class. The feedback is immediate and precise and begins with questions. In what ways does the writer show rather than tell? Are there places in the writing where it needs more showing and less telling? How might the writer accomplish that? The process does not involve taking papers home to grade. To give you an idea about what happens with this approach, we include two telling sentences and student responses.

Telling Sentence: The drive in the car was uncomfortable.

Sitting in the back seat of the small economy car while driving through the hot and humid desert was a miserable experience. The 110-degree weather along with the 80 percent humidity added somewhat to the stickiness of the situation. Though the seven of us were squished together, we managed to entertain ourselves by letting the sweat run down our bodies and dribble to our feet. (p. 27)

This small paragraph is packed with specific details. The writer substitutes the telling word *uncomfortable* for a less ambiguous description: *the back seat of the small economy car*. Using a series of numbers—*110, 80, seven*—the writer illustrates misery and stickiness. The verbs (*squished, dribble*) serve as photos for the reader, along with the visual image of sweat making its way down to the feet.

Telling Sentence: My room was a mess.

To enter the room, I was forced to squeeze in the small door opening, nearly getting stuck because heaps of dirty clothes obstructed the path of the door. Once inside, I had to concentrate fully on every step so that my shoes wouldn't become tangled in the laundry and cause me to fall. Steps later, after freeing my leg from a malicious pair of blue corduroy pants, I noticed that under the spot vacated by those pants was a matted piece of green shag carpet, the only piece of carpet not being smothered by clothing in the entire room. . . . I flung myself on the bed, long parted with its sheets, and wondered if I wouldn't be safer waiting in another room. (p. 31)

This little gem demonstrates several "show not tell" techniques. Note the effective active verbs—*squeeze, obstructed, tangled, smothered, flung*—and the appropriate, well-chosen visual details—*heaps of dirty clothes*, *freeing my leg*, *smothered by clothing*, *long parted with its sheets*. The writer has also successfully bestowed human characteristics on an inanimate object: *a malicious pair of blue corduroy pants*.

No matter how students practice "show not tell," they will benefit from some kind of classroom or Google Docs exchange. Time permitting, students can display their papers with a digital projector or read their papers to a small group. Alternatively, students can trade papers, underline the showing details, and make suggestions for additional specifics. It's also useful for students to name "show not tell" strategies, using labels like the ones below:

- Appropriate adjectives
- Active verbs
- Intentional and selective description
- Bestowing human characteristics on inanimate objects
- Specific details
- Comparing or contrasting
- Examples/illustrations
- Elaboration
- Re-creating an experience
- Proper nouns
- Characterizations
- Meaningful dialogue
- Revealing a character's inner thoughts (Murphy & Smith, 2015)

You may notice that these strategies work for narrative and other kinds of writing as well. True! Learning them in one genre like narrative makes them available in others—just as learning to write narrative makes it available and useful in other genres.

CHAPTER 4

Writing for Poetic Effect

Like narrative, poetry often gets a pink slip early on in school, hardly ever to return except possibly as a form to be studied and sometimes imitated, its lines counted and parsed. Ah, the sonnet, the ballad, the ode!

Poetry, however, is one of the few genres that gives students the chance to play with language. It's the every-word-counts kind of writing, one that also allows students to go against rules, take shortcuts, and escape from formulas. It calls on students to use their imaginations, sometimes a rarity in our breaking news world where information is king. And with poetry, students can front-load their own experiences.

Writing poetry is an engaging, fast-track, and personal way for students to advance their language skills and literacy talents—skills that transfer to other forms of writing. The kinds of language students learn when they experiment with poetry are pervasive across disciplines. Take figurative language in science, for example:

> Metaphors in biology and ecology are so ubiquitous that we have to some extent become blind to their existence. We are inundated with metaphorical language, such as genetic "blueprints," ecological "footprints," "invasive" species, "agents" of infectious disease, "superbugs," "food chains," "missing links," and so on. (Taylor & Dewsbury, 2018, para. 8)

Taylor and Dewsbury (2018) go so far as to say it's not just language that comes into play with figures of speech: "metaphors are not just linguistic embellishments. Rather, they are foundations for thought processes and conceptual understandings" (para. 5).

When poetry sneaks back into the classroom, it can "become a gateway to other forms of writing":

> It can help teach skills that come in handy with other kinds of writing—like precise, economical diction, for example. When Carl Sandburg writes, "The fog comes/on little cat feet," in just six words, he endows a natural phenomenon with character, a pace, and a spirit. All forms of writing benefit from the powerful and concise phrases found in poems. (Simmons, 2014, para. 7)

As we feature it in this chapter, poetry rolls out a red carpet for students to explore their language, culture, and identity—the very parts of themselves that are often parked outside the school building. If these personal connections stay on the sidelines, literacy learning itself is hampered. As Ann Marie Smith (2010) explains, "literacy is more than writing words; literacy learning is tied up with identities, cultural expectations and rhetorical situations" (p. 215). Plus, poetry invites all comers: "Poetry is for everyone and [through] poetry our students' lives—'the landscape and bread' of their homes, their ancestors, their struggles and joys—are invited into classrooms as subjects worthy of study" (Christensen & Watson, 2015, p. 3).

Writing poetry also lends itself to multimodal productions—another way to bring the student's world into the classroom and to give students new literacy tools that move audiences to action or understanding. Just as we can throw open the school door and usher in personal experiences and identities through poetry, we can welcome in a broader range of literacies. Poetry offers "creative applications of new media that build on the literacies students have already developed outside of school through their immersion in digital technologies" (Hughes, 2007, p. 1).

ABOUT THIS CHAPTER:
WHAT COMES FROM WRITING POEMS

Here, we return to Emma Richardson, who teaches poetry and poetic language to 12th-graders, students who are often subject to an endless barrage of literary analysis and informational and argumentative writing. Her focus on poetic writing, her emphasis on precise, evocative words and images, underscores language that makes an impact in all kinds of writing. As Richardson says, "I stress that the best prose is poetic prose" (personal communication, October 28, 2019). Richardson wants her students to bankroll as many poetic writing strategies as possible to use whenever or with whatever they write.

Richardson's second classroom closeup (see the first one in Chapter 3) concentrates on a single poetry assignment, one that calls for students to celebrate their language and identity. Her students' writing illustrates how poems "illuminate our lives and breathe new life, new seeing, new tasting into the world we thought we knew" (Housden, 2011).

Poet Claudia Rankine (2004) writes poems that address incidents of racism in our everyday interactions. In the second part of the chapter, we look at the power of her multigenre and multimodal poems as they defy the usual ideas about what a poem should look like, address contemporary social issues, and provide models for students to experiment with making an impact on their own communities through poetry.

CLASSROOM CLOSEUP: LANGUAGE AND IDENTITY
#speechways #celebratelanguage

When Richardson stresses poems and poetic writing, she gives her students the very resources they need to write effectively in all kinds of situations. The idea that students will transfer learning from one occasion to another is a long-held notion in education. For example, we hope students will bring with them what they learned from one writing task to the next. Richardson does not settle for hope. She consciously teaches students language skills that are portable from poetry to prose, and she supports repurposing these skills in other contexts like the college application essay. Yancey, Robertson, and Taczak (2014) emphasize that "if we want students to transfer, we have to teach *for* it" (p. 7). We might add that this kind of teaching gives lessons like Richardson's poetic writing more meaning and impact because the learning is not a once-only event. When nurtured, it has a ripple effect, showing up on all kinds of writing occasions.

> Yet, it is true, poetry is delicious; the best prose is that which is most full of poetry.
> —Virginia Woolf

But there's even more to bringing poetry into the classroom. Richardson's poetry assignments and lessons invite students to connect their lives outside of school to the writing they do on the inside. Notice how the task below asks students to play with their own language, and at the same time, play with poetic language:

> Write a poem that celebrates the "speech ways" of your home or home community.
>
> You might begin by making a list of words or phrases you hear at home, words or phrases that are "easy on your ear" while you're in that familiar place, but perhaps are words or phrases that you don't necessarily hear or use outside your home or community.
>
> Who uses those words? When you think of them, do you also recall people's faces or the timbre of their voices? In your "mind's eye," do you see a setting, a place, where those words are spoken? Offer images that communicate those things.
>
> You could write the entire poem about one word or phrase, or you could integrate several words or phrases into your poem. (Personal communication, August 20, 2019)

Right off the bat, this assignment offers choice and personal connection. It has the potential to produce writing that evokes an emotion, that will be meaningful and culturally relevant to both writer and reader, and that will get high marks for passion. The language of the assignment encourages imagination: "in your 'mind's eye'" and "recall people's faces or the timbre of their voices."

We don't pretend that every student will find inspiration from every assignment, no matter how well designed. Richardson is banking on connection to home, family, country, and identity—connections that students are likely to make. She points her students to language—recalling it, hearing and seeing it, claiming it as your own, and celebrating it as the pride and special character of your people. In choosing language as the focus, Richardson engineers the odds that the topic will matter to students, since language is so central to who we are.

Here is an example of what Richardson is shooting for, with its sounds and sights:

Di'lects

By Aiden Dunkelberg

The old woman spoke a language foreign to my father's ears,
A dialect unbeknownst to the ears of corn
He grew up surrounded by.
Unknown to the heart of the Heartland,
Small-town northern Iowa,
With its golden summers and subzero winters.
But it was the language
My mother had grown up with,
That rolled through the hills and valleys of her childhood.
The language of y'all and yes, ma'am and a thousand
Stereotypical phrases but in her home
It was the things you didn't expect that my father noticed:
Like "making" a picture, gettin' into "the" bed,
"Liking" cantaloupe for dinner because you didn't
Get up in time to run down to Henley's and fetch some.
It's a language I grew up with,
Simmered in like butter beans in boiling water,
And maybe I don't speak it all the time
But it fits my mouth and teeth and tongue
Like a well-worn glove that slips onto my fingers.
So that when we pull into the carport
Of my grandmother's low-slung brick ranch house
And she comes out to ask,
"Did y'all make it alright?"
I can answer yes, ma'am in a watered-down
Facsimile of her own peculiar mix
Of Appalachian drawl and Deep South lilt
Just different enough to be homage and not mimicry.

Because sure, globalization is a good thing,
But our accents and our cultures are retreating,
And if there's one thing I've noticed
I can only sound like her when I'm talking to her.

In terms of *writing to make an impact*, this poem speaks for itself. It speaks in the language of the grandmother. It speaks with images like "butter beans in boiling water" and "a well-worn glove that slips onto my fingers." It speaks of "y'alls" that are attached to a time, a place, and a special person.

This piece could have been an essay about preserving language and culture. The form it takes—a poem with its "powerful and concise phrases"—illustrates the power of this genre for the student who owns it and for the reader who enters the world of "Appalachian drawl and Deep South lilt."

POETRY AND NARRATIVE
#setting #characters #scenes

In many cases, poetry has elements of narrative—people, places, and events. Richardson's language assignment opens up opportunities for students to focus on such elements. Notice in the poem below the interweaving of homeland and new land, the contrasting of scenes and voices.

American Dream
By Roy Wrishija

Lowndes County is 8,471 miles away
from the country where I was born.
My culture and memories of Bangladesh
stretch beyond the distance separating us,
continuing to influence me just as my
Southern American neighborhood does.
And yet, Mississippi is the place I call home.

Potholes dipping into crack tar and towering
Mississippi magnolias replace narrow, muddy
streets and looming mango trees.
Rhythmic taps of soulful blues music drown
out harsh bangs of fast-paced tabla drums.
My piano teacher's Southern drawl challenges
the musical dynamic of my Ma's and Baba's voices.
The crispy smell of catfish replaces the spicy,
mustard-infused curry of Bangladeshi fishing villages.

When someone says "Mississippi," many
may think of sweltering heat rays and
fist-sized mosquitoes, or some may think of
the stars and stripes crisscrossing to make
the Confederate flag.

I see more than these shortcomings. I see
Open pastures populated with horses and cows,
see immense loblolly pine forests. I see
chilly glasses of lemon-infused sweet tea
beside crumbly cornbread. I see
my multiracial friends laughing; I see MSMS, a
school providing me with intensive labs
and in-depth perspectives on literature, see
calculus theorems and chemistry concepts,
all nurturing my passions.
This is the American Dream.
This is my Mississippi.

In a poem loaded with sensory images of language, food, and music, the narrator portrays his transition from one world to another. Some of the images illustrate the challenges of changing cultures, of the barriers to fitting into this new place—"sweltering heat rays," and "stars and stripes crisscrossing to make the Confederate flag." In the end, the narrator comes to appreciate the beauty and benefits of his new surroundings: "lemon-infused sweet tea," "my multiracial friends laughing," "in-depth perspectives."

> I've always tried to think of poetry as an active ingredient in the language rather than just something that appears between the covers of thin books.
> —Simon Armitage

The poem offers glimpses of setting and characters; it's packed with specifics and stunning visuals—"looming mango trees" and "fist-sized mosquitos." It's solidly connected to this student's life experience. Plus, it comes with another a big bonus for the student: It provides a chance to experiment with and learn about poetic writing. All the rest of Roy's writing will likely benefit, as Andrew Simmons (2014) has suggested, from this immersion into "the powerful and concise phrases found in poems" (para. 7).

It's worth noting exactly what's in the "bank" for this young writer, the techniques he's used here that are portable and available for his next writing event:

- Specific details: Lowndes County is 8,471 miles away
- Sensory images: crispy smell of catfish, mustard-infused curry
- Proper nouns: Lowndes County, Bangladesh, Mississippi, Ma, Baba
- Active verbs: stretch, replace, drown out, challenges

Alliteration: Mississippi magnolias, crumbly cornbread

 Repetition for effect: I see, I see, I see

 Participles: Potholes dipping, sweltering heat rays, towering magnolias

POETRY OR PROSE OR WHAT?

#multigenre #multimodal

Jamaican poet Claudia Rankine (2004) blends poetry, prose, and photos into pieces that capture injustices in the world our students live in right now. Her poems are inventive, energetic combinations of words and visual images, the kind of communication that is right up the alley of today's student. And yet, Rankine's poems are not tweets or Snapchats or hip-hop or rap. Nor do they look like poems.

This excerpt from *Don't Let Me Be Lonely: An American Lyric* (2004) illustrates the hybrid nature of Rankine's poetry:

> At the airport-security checkpoint on my way to visit my grandmother, I am asked to drink from my water bottle.
>
> This water bottle?
>
> That's right. Open it and drink from it.
>
> At the airport-security checkpoint on my way to visit my grandmother, I am asked to take off my shoes.
>
> Take off my shoes?
>
> Yes. Both Please.
>
> At the airport-security checkpoint on my way to visit my grandmother, I am asked if I have a fever.
>
> A fever? Really?
>
> Yes. Really.
>
> My grandmother is in a nursing home. It's not bad. It doesn't smell like pee. It doesn't smell like anything. When I go to see her, as I walk through the hall past the common room and the nurses' station, old person after old person puts out his or her hand to me. Steven, one says. Ann, another calls. It's like being in a third-world country, but instead of food or money you are what is wanted, your company. (pp. 105–108)

In this poem, Rankine highlights her time in a TSA line and her walk through the hall of her grandmother's nursing home, two experiences she has pared back to bits of dialogue and images of hand after hand reaching out to her in the nursing home. "It's like being in a third-world country …" she writes, a phrase that connects one experience to the other.

The contemporary look and feel of Rankine's poems distinguish them from poems with verse, meter, and rhyme. Her work is like theater, with characters and talk. But here's a legitimate question that is bound to come up when we think about crowding one more thing into an already overstuffed curriculum: "What can multimodal poetry possibly do for students that would make it worth the time?" Tom Charles (2008) writes that his English learners who experimented with a multimodal approach to poetry not only "used the poetry to expand and explore their own views of the world" but their "use and knowledge of the English language increased" (p. 3). Daniel Xerri (2012) encourages us to tap into students' visual and digital literacy skills, citing his own experiences when doing so. His students were able to "create video poems, podcasts, hypertext and Wikis, all of which represent new ways of using language and experiencing poetry" (p. 507). Probably the most compelling reason comes from Mark Dressman and Celia Genishi (2010): "We live in a multimodal world, in which the most influential and pervasive texts . . . are likely to be those that combine print with still images, video, and sound in exciting ways" (p. 105).

Rankine's poems, then, offer another way that writing in school can carry an impact, especially when it's in line with the kinds of literacy students are already engaged in. We explore an idea for helping students put Rankine's crossbreed brand on their own poetry in the teaching playbook.

THE TAKEAWAYS

- In addition to providing a pathway for language development, experimentation, and transferrable skills, poetry is also a medium for exploring experience. Assignments like Richardson's accomplish all of these.
- Poetry lends itself to invention and collaboration. The teaching playbook activities that follow emphasize having students work together to discover language and shared and/or distinctive life experiences, cultures, identities—especially important for English language learners—but also for all of us.
- Poetry does not have to look like, well, poetry. It can look like prose poetry, like the vibrancy of poetic language in other kinds of writing, like the poetry in songs and chants. It easily slips out of English classes. Try the blockbuster *Hamilton* as one example.
- Economy and precision of language—signature features of poetry—are at the heart of the mission statements McWilliams's students write for their Humanitarian Projects (Chapter 2). You will find the same call for precision in elevator pitches—a genre that features prominently in the civic engagement projects in the next chapter.
- Poetry is contagious. It spreads its impact broadly on the language we use, on our feelings and our ways of seeing things. It improvises and

attracts new literacies. It gives permission for our students to write about what matters to them in a way that matters to them.

TEACHING PLAYBOOK

Zeroing in on Active Verbs—Word Walls and Notebooks

We start with Linda Christensen for this generative activity, which focuses on teaching students to recognize and use active verbs, the movers and shakers in poems and in all kinds of writing. Christensen (2009) tells her class, "Verbs make your poetry (and essays) strut and dance, or they make your audience snore" (p. 44).

> Verbs make your poetry (and essays) strut and dance, or they make your audience snore.
> —Linda Christensen

She begins by showcasing sports poems because verbs "dominate the pieces" (p. 44), reading them aloud, and asking students to highlight the verbs. Here are some lively poems you might consider:

Recommended by Linda Christensen (p. 45):

"A Poem for Magic" by Quincy Troupe: betterlivingthroughbeowulf.com/take-it-to-the-hoop-magic-johnson/
"Analysis of Baseball" by Mae Swenson: www.poetryfoundation.org/poems/48193/analysis-of-baseball
"Fast Break" by Edward Hirsch: poets.org/poem/fast-break
"The Base Stealer" by Robert Francis: www.poemhunter.com/poem/the-base-stealer/

Other recommendations:

"A Boy Juggling a Soccer Ball" by Christopher Merrill: poets.org/poem/boy-juggling-soccer-ball
"Slam, Dunk, & Hook" by Yusef Komunyakaa: www.poetryfoundation.org/poems/50245/slam-dunk-hook
"Makin' Jump Shots" by Michael S. Harper: www.poetryfoundation.org/poems/53470/makin-jump-shots
"Evening Practice" by D. Nurkse: www.poetryfoundation.org/poems/49042/evening-practice
"Wide Receiver" by Mark Halliday: www.poetryfoundation.org/poems/57656/wide-receiver

As a slight variation on Christensen's next steps, we suggest you work together with the class to create a list of things people do in the world, such as cook, sing, dance, run, paint, or play any sport. Then, with partners or in small groups, students pick one they like and brainstorm active verbs that fit with the activity. For example, if students choose "sing," their list of active verbs might look like this: *warble, croon, harmonize, belt out, bellow out, purr, chirp, chant, hum, call, whistle, drone.*

The last step is to have students post their lists on a word wall. By posting language in this way, students create a print-rich environment that belongs to them. They own the wall. Equally important, the word wall is alive, organic, and dynamic. Students can add to it over time, and in the case of poetic writing, they can add images, metaphors, and other sensory words and phrases. They can also keep lists in their notebooks as a personal collection that is right there whenever they need it.

Spotlighting one feature of poetic language like active verbs, giving that feature prominence in reading and writing activities, posting samples around the classroom—these are strategies that make the feature accessible and ready to go for students. Any of the features like sensory images, proper nouns, and alliteration in Roy Wrishija's "American Dream" poem work for this kind of practice.

Creating Images: Revisiting "Show Don't Tell"

Recall the teaching playbook in Chapter 3 with "show don't tell" exercises for narrative writing. One advantage of poetry is that the "showing" can be abbreviated—no complete sentences required—and it can come in the form of a list.

We believe in lists: lists of people and places, lists of significant events and turning points. What better way to come up with ideas for our narratives, our arguments, and yes, our poems?

For this exercise, we have adapted a first-rate activity Michael McGriff (2015) created for the Poetry Foundation. We especially like this activity because it is unbounded by any genre, allowing students to give all their attention to the idea of exploring and recalling images.

The activity starts with a list. McGriff suggests coming up with at least 50 objects that have personal significance. The possibilities are wide open. Students can list the family kitchen table at the same time they list a baseball mitt or a pair of fuzzy nighttime socks or a book at their bedside. You might want to try it out yourself to share the experience with your students.

Step two is to list memories, at least 20, that match the objects. For example, you might remember a Thanksgiving dinner around a familiar table, or a championship game when a baseball mitt does its duty with the winning catch.

The penultimate step is to select a memory or two and list all the sensory images the writer can remember. And there is the blueprint for a poem.

Our adaptations take into account the way lists can serve so many purposes so well. Depending on where or when this lesson fits into your curriculum, you might want to consider one of these list possibilities. For example, what about lists of culturally significant objects? Lists of friends, family members, allies? Lists of tools, games, technologies? Lists of things I can't get along without? Music lists? Lists of journeys or geographies? Lists of animals and food and cars?

Think lists. Some teachers focus the lists on place: What's in your closet or on your kitchen counter? What's on your "dream" list?

Images are easier to come by when students establish a setting or a set of circumstances. The brilliance of McGriff's lesson is that it does both. Keep in mind that the goal is to roll out a list of images—however you frame the lead-in.

Lists come naturally to most of us. We use them to organize, remember, and prompt ourselves to get things done. We make wish lists and bucket lists. Lists give us structure. They also help us make sense of the world. The lists we recommend here build language, personal connections, and content for writing. To the extent that they can bring poetry from the outskirts into the curriculum, they may give students much-needed practice and (gasp) *fun* with language.

Bringing Students' Lives into the Classroom: Identity Poems

Both Richardson and Christensen invite students to write about their lives, their cultures, and their identities. Richardson's task centers on language, "speech ways" of her students' home, family, and community. Christensen (2018) picks up on a similar theme with "Where I'm From" poems. She begins by having her students read "Where I'm From" by George Ella Lyon, a poem she uses "to invite my students' families, homes, and neighborhoods into the classroom." Here's a look at the first two lines (for the complete poem, see teacher.scholastic.com/writeit/PDF/lyon.pdf):

I am from clothespins,
from Clorox and carbon-tetrachloride.

The centerpiece of Christensen's (2018) lesson is having students collect images from their own worlds that match those in Lyon's poem: items found around their home, in their yard, in their neighborhood, names of relatives, foods, dishes, places, and so on. Once again, lists provide the starting gate for a poem, and in this case, students have a model and a structure to follow. In addition to being the grist for the poem they will write, these lists all by themselves provide a "space for their [students'] lives to become part of the curriculum" (para. 9).

Inviting students to bring their life experiences into the classroom is part of a long tradition of student-centered instruction. One early and prominent advocate, John Dewey (1907), urged teachers to connect curriculum to the interests of students to make learning more effective. More recently, the focus is on culturally relevant teaching, which also characterizes Christensen's approach.

The term "culturally relevant" comes from the groundbreaking work of Gloria Ladson-Billings (1995), who identified key tenets to guide teachers in using "students' culture as a vehicle for learning" (p.161). Ladson-Billings's ideas have reverberated over several decades. More recently, Knight-Manuel and Marciano (2019) define culturally relevant education as "a conceptual framework that recognizes the importance of including students' cultural backgrounds, interests, and lived experiences in all aspects of teaching and learning within the classroom and across the school" (p. 4).

For more detailed information about Christensen's approach to student identity and identity poems, see www.ateq.org/where-im-from-inviting-student-lives-into-the-classroom.html.

Combining Poetry, Narrative, and Visual Images

For this generation of students, Claudia Rankine sheds new light on what's possible in poetry in terms of content (poems about race) and of form.

Here are some thoughts about using Rankine's poems as a touchstone for students to write their own prose poems:

First, sift through lots of Rankine poems, her stories about injustices and how people hurt each other. These are also well worth the time to discuss, along with asking questions about how injustices come to be.

Students will have their own stories about injustices, humiliations, or micro-aggressions—intentional or unintentional comments that subtly demean someone in a marginalized group. These stories can become the content of poems if students are comfortable revisiting them. Or they can select other stories as the starting point, perhaps ones about a challenge, frustration, or triumph.

Students can write their prose poems without worrying about line breaks. They can roam freely from words to pictures. The tricky part is to curate the story, boil it down to the bits that are absolutely necessary, and do the same with words. Every word, every verbal or visual image, has to perform and lead to the next. All this takes mindful attention to meaning and associations.

If you want to give poetry an even more expansive liftoff, you can encourage students to take it beyond the printed page to video, dramatic readings, dance, role-play, or improvisation. Dressman and Genishi (2010) advocate for doing something active and concrete with poems:

[M]ark them for a choral reading, write and play with them on paper, sing them as the blues, write them for reading and performance, or remix them multimodally. These activities push students to use not only their minds but also their bodies and an expanding repertoire of cultural practices. (p. 104)

Whether or not you use Rankine as a model, having students find open-ended models for their own writing, tell their own stories, and bring up their own issues is a good thing, a way to marry words and impact. We encourage you to test-drive some of the options here and see what comes from them.

CHAPTER 5

Writing to Take Action

Years ago, before all the attention to healthy eating, a friend of ours went to a PTA meeting at his child's elementary school. He wanted to make a pitch for an addition to the school's weekly "hot dog" day menu: a turkey hot dog. Because the regular beef hot dog contained artificial colors and flavors, his allergic son always missed out on the coveted meal. Our friend thought his request seemed reasonable, and even enlightened—a no-child-left-behind kind of action. He never anticipated the backlash to his proposal. Bear in mind that at that time the turkey hot dog was a relatively new phenomenon, one that looked limp and gray, and frankly (excuse our pun) distasteful. The other parents were enraged by the very thought of turkey side-by-side with beef. "What's wrong with a good old hot dog?" they demanded. A voice from the back of the room shouted, "Turkey hot dog? That's un-American!" In the end, our friend prevailed, although he told us he would never go to another PTA meeting, nor would he speak up for a turkey hot dog again in his life.

As our friend learned, calling for action takes knowing what to do, where to start, whom to talk to, what to say, and how to say it. At the minimum, you need the right language, a set of strategies, a willingness to be vulnerable, and, yes, a thick skin. These abilities don't just show up one day. They take work and practice and probably a few near-misses like the turkey hot dog adventure.

For students, learning to see themselves as agents of change is a step toward using *writing to make an impact* in their communities. To take action successfully, they have to identify problems and imagine they can be part of the solution. In the process, they may discover the benefits of technology beyond the selfie when they use technology as a tool to learn more about their communities and to reach out responsibly to transform them (Delgado, 2017).

Civic engagement or civic action has become something of a catchphrase these days. What is it exactly, and who gets engaged? From our conversations with teachers and students and from our own experience, we have put together this description of a civic action project. In general, it asks students to do the following:

- Work on a real issue
- Conduct research, including firsthand inquiries such as surveys, interviews, and/or focus groups
- Develop a position or proposal, including a way to proceed
- Advocate for and defend positions through face-to-face and digital activities
- Write and speak "using a public voice" in various genres, such as presentations, petitions, short pitches, podcasts, letters, emails, blogs, videos, and/or public service announcements

Outside of the classroom, we hear calls to action in some way every day—whether in a tweet or talk show or blog. The air we breathe swirls with responses to social conditions, pressures, and realities. By bringing students into the mix, teachers give them a crack at learning how to respond responsibly and effectively to the social forces around them. Engaging in civic issues in some way can be part of a student's job—a job that comes with excellent benefits, according to Christine Cress (2012):

> Don't ask kids what they want to be when they grow up but what problems do they want to solve.
> —Jaime Cassap

> As a strategic educational approach, civic engagement works. Thoughtful and purposefully designed civic engagement activities yield greater learning and increased graduation rates in K–12 schools, community colleges, and four-year institutions (Astin et al., 2006; Bridgeland, DiIulio, & Morison 2006; Prentice & Robinson 2010). In fact, Gent (2007) has argued that civic engagement is one way to ensure that no student is left behind. (2012, para. 7)

Engaging in civic learning has monumental payoffs for students, according to the *Civic Mission of Schools* report by the Carnegie Corporation (2003). Students are:

- more likely to vote and discuss politics at home,
- four times more likely to volunteer and work on community issues, and
- more confident in their ability to speak publicly and communicate with their elected representatives.

In addition, "Students who receive both traditional and interactive civics score highest on assessments and demonstrate high levels of twenty-first century skills such as critical thinking, news comprehension, and work ethic" (p. 7).

ABOUT THIS CHAPTER:
EDUCATING FOR DEMOCRACY WITH CIVIC ENGAGEMENT

In this chapter, we illustrate how a civic engagement project invites students into the adult world of writing, the kind of writing that gets things done. This is writing that challenges an audience to take an action or adopt a point of view; at the same time, this is writing that challenges a young writer to be precise and accurate with facts, to make an effective case, to use a public voice, and to reach outside the classroom for an audience.

Civic action writing in school is practice for now and for the future, a point Stan Pesick makes about its value: "If they [students] choose to write letters to the editor or read the newspaper or have a discussion with somebody, they are better prepared to do those things as adults. An even bigger purpose is engaging students with a wider audience, something they seldom have a chance to do." (All Pesick quotes in this chapter are from a personal communication, November 7, 2017.)

We will look in detail at one civic engagement effort with a group of Oakland 9th-graders: the Take Action Project. Their English and history teacher, Matt Colley, claims: "Civic engagement work has given students a sense of agency, a sense of voice, and a structure to think about 'how can I actually do something with the things that I'm learning.'" According to Colley, students also come to "really see school as a springboard to community engagement, as opposed to a report card grade" (quoted in "How civic engagement helps students see their capacity to make change," 2016).

Here, we concentrate on exploring and unpacking the writing opportunities Colley offers his class focusing on these:

- Petition
- Elevator pitch
- Call for action
- Reflection

As we know, collaborative long-term projects ask a lot of students. Just keeping up some kind of momentum can be a stretch. But a long-term project that requires adolescents to do real-world activities—something they may not have experienced before—poses even more challenges. So we talked to the kids themselves: a group from Colley's class and a group from Judy Kennedy's 12th-grade government class.

> There is all the difference in the world between having something to say and having to say something.
>
> —John Dewey

Kennedy, a social studies teacher in San Lorenzo, California, has 7 years of experience with civic action projects. The issues these students raise are applicable to many long-term projects that students tackle in school—for example,

McWilliams's Humanitarian Project in Chapter 2 and two projects you will read about in Chapter 7. The student comments from both classes confirm that students recognize the benefits of engaging in civic action even as they complain about the demands of long-term projects.

As always, we finish the chapter with some teaching ideas, particularly those that relate to process, and also a list of resources.

CLASSROOM CLOSEUP: TEACHING STUDENTS HOW TO TAKE ACTION
#writingtoadvocate #bigtimebenefits

Several years ago, Matt Colley and 90 of his colleagues participated in a district- and National Writing Project–sponsored initiative called Educating for Democracy in the Digital Age (2012–2016). Young Wan Choi, former teacher and district leader, coordinated the initiative and supported the group as its members developed strategies to engage students in addressing controversial issues. Colley's story is a testimony to what happens when teachers have time to work together for the benefit of their students.

In Colley's 9th-grade class, students collaborated on civic action projects and in the process learned to see writing in a new way, including:

- the kinds of writing that advocates use;
- the role of writing in addressing a problem and calling for action; and
- the shift in audience, from classmates to the larger public.

THE ROLE OF AN ADVOCATE
#jobdescription

The first order of business for Colley is to situate his students in a role that is, for most, novel and maybe a bit daunting. In order to be effective advocates, students need to consider the following questions:

- Who is your target audience? Is this an audience that has the authority to do something about the problem?
- What more do you need to learn about the problem? What kinds of research do you need to do?
- What part of the problem is within your grasp? How will you explain/demonstrate that part?
- What exactly will you ask your audience (and yourself) to do about the problem?
- By what means will you persuade your audience to act? What tactics will you use?

- Who is going to be on your team? (You probably don't want to go solo like the turkey dog guy.)
- What organizations or individuals are already working on the issue?

Obviously, these are not questions for a worksheet. Civic engagement projects tax students who are looking for easy, unambiguous answers. Finding the right target audience or tactic, for example, might take more trial and error than students usually have to endure. So how interested might they be in taking on the complex role of an advocate, including the writing that will be involved?

According to Colley, the writing students do as advocates is "inherently engaging for them. They want to be listened to. They want to persuade someone. They are willing to put in the time." (All Matt Colley quotes are from a personal communication on January 29, 2018, unless otherwise noted.)

> Never be afraid to raise your voice for honesty and truth and compassion against injustice and lying and greed. If people all over the world . . . would do this, it would change the earth.
>
> —William Faulkner

It seems that Colley's students are not alone. A 2016 survey of 141,189 full-time, first-year college students from around the United States found that interest in political and civic engagement has reached the highest levels since the ongoing study began 50 years ago. The survey was conducted by the Higher Education Research Institute and the UCLA Graduate School of Education and Information Studies:

> Further demonstrating students' interest in community engagement, 39.8 percent of incoming freshmen said they want to become community leaders, while 60 percent expressed strong interest in improving their understanding of other countries and cultures—in both cases, the highest figures ever for those survey questions. In addition, 22.3 percent of students hope to influence the political structure and 41.2 percent say that helping to promote racial understanding is either an "essential" or "very important" personal goal. ("College students' commitment to activism," 2016)

TEACHING CIVIC ENGAGEMENT TACTICS
#petitionsforchange

Colley introduces his students to a variety of genres—posters, petitions, fliers, infographics, boycotts, oral histories, presentations—and has them try out some of these in preparation for their projects. For example, students learn about petitions by creating them collaboratively around some issue connected to the school. The most promising ones become the work of the whole class, with everyone pitching in to revise, edit, and create a complete package, including infographics.

One year, Colley's history classes focused on eliminating the Body Mass Index (BMI) as a part of the school's required physical fitness test. The BMI—a key index to relate weight to height—is a way of quantifying the amount of muscle, fat, and bone in an individual and then designating the individual as underweight, normal weight, overweight, or obese. Students argued that the BMI may give a false impression (for example, a healthy muscular person might have a high BMI). But closer to home, the students associated the BMI with body shaming and objected to the consequences if they "failed" the BMI. As you read this excerpt from the students' petition, notice that each paragraph performs a particular duty in outlining the students' concerns.

Get Rid of the BMI

The requirements for passing the 9th grade Physical Fitness Test need to be changed. The Body Composition portion should be removed entirely because the Body Mass Index, or BMI test is unfair, racist, fatphobic, and inaccurate. Although the composition tests are used to help students become healthy and not obese, it is not a healthy practice to pass or fail students based on their weight.

Every single student who goes through the public school system is familiar with the Physical Fitness Test. It tests our upper body strength, our aerobic capacity, and a variety of other athletic skills. It also tests our BMI. However, the BMI test is unfair. For students with a high muscle mass, it sometimes classifies them as overweight when they're at a perfectly healthy weight, and for overweight students, they'll be forced to run the mile faster in order to pass, which is often not a possible feat for those students. Thus, they fail PE class and have to take it the next year, taking up an academic slot that could have gone to a STEM class they were passionate about, or a language class that would connect them to their ancestry, or just any class they needed to graduate. Having your weight decide how likely it is you'll pass the PFT is a toxic practice that promotes fatphobia. . . .

The last thing young people need is for the media representation of bodies to be brought into the school environment. Imagine literally failing your body test: it would make you feel like you body is a failure and your body is not beautiful, and like it's your fault and you need to fix it. The BMI test calls students out in class for their flaws rather than focusing on how to live a healthy lifestyle. I know personally how self conscious and body image obsessed teens can be, and having a test that measures your body in school causes even more comparison between peers, and society's unrealistic expectations. By having the BMI test in school we are perpetuating self-confidence issues and negativity to accepting all body types. The BMI test does not belong in school. (Get Rid of the BMI, n.d.)

The headline cuts to the chase, previewing what the students want to change. The first paragraph reiterates the call for action with a concise explanation of the issue and explains why it deserves immediate attention. A more detailed explanation appears in the following paragraph, with information about how the BMI test might be unfair, inaccurate, or in some way damaging to a student's academic goals. The emotional plea shows up in the last part of this excerpt. The writers make a direct appeal to their audience: "Imagine literally failing your body test. . . ." They suggest that the test is not only damaging to a young person's self-image and confidence, but that it targets the wrong thing. The emphasis should be on learning how to live a healthy lifestyle.

This "practice" petition introduces students to an unfamiliar genre before they tackle their own civic action projects. But it's not just practice for the sake of practice. Ultimately, the petition goes live on Change.org. Posting petitions makes the writing for real. Students have called upon an audience to take an action; they have made a case about a problem that is worth addressing.

Solidifying the Issue
#boilingthingsdown #reasonablerequests

Colley is a realist about the Take Action Project. It gives students "a sense of ownership and power and optimism." At the same time, so much depends on trimming a project to a manageable size. Students have a tendency to select huge problems that are beyond their reach—problems like poverty, hunger, or violence that will not be solved by a petition, no matter how well written. For a petition to do its job, students have to come up with a reasonable request and address an audience that can do something about the issue.

> Petitions solidify civic action thinking.
> —Matt Colley

Take a look at excerpts from the first and last paragraphs of a petition addressed to the school district superintendent about a way to mitigate problems of sexual discrimination and harassment on campuses:

We, the signatories of this petition demand that the Oakland Unified School District implements a Title IX coordinator for *each school* whose sole job is to enforce the district's compliance with Title IX, as required by federal law. Currently, [the district] is neglecting its duty to provide its students with Title IX coordinators for each school, and instead has one to represent all complaints of over 48,000 students, thus creating an unsafe and unjust environment for all students, especially those who are female and/or a part of the LGBTQ+ community. . . . (Stop Sexual Assault in Oakland Unified School District, 2017)

This is a request that is within the realm of possibility. It appeals to an audience that has some authority to initiate action. It doesn't attempt to rid the world of sexual harassment. Rather, it takes the problem down to a local level with the potential to improve the situation. In the following excerpt from one of the last paragraphs, the writers spell out the benefits of the proposed action:

Through implementing a qualified Title IX Coordinator to take charge of the each school's sexual harassment complaints and work towards educating the students and staff on sex discrimination, [the district] would be working transformatively toward an environment in which every student truly could thrive. A Title IX coordinator would provide students filing a sexual harassment case with necessary timeliness, care, and expertise, which is lacking in the current system. . . . Additionally the coordinator would provide a) a clear way of contacting them to the students and staff, thus eliminating the many unreported incidents of sexual harassment going on in our schools, b) clear distribution of the district's policy against sex discrimination to diffuse current confusion on policies, c) ensurance of less sex discrimination in our schools, and d) an increased education on sex discrimination in order to end the continuation of sexual harassment in schools. (Stop Sexual Assault in Oakland Unified School District, 2017)

This paragraph illustrates that students have caught on to the genre Colley has taught them. The writers have attempted to be concise, convincing, and clear. They have mixed information, persuasion, and emotional appeal to persuade the superintendent to take a specific action.

We would also suggest that something significant has happened for the students themselves. For their voices to be heard, they have had to learn how to shape a demand and give it a rationale. They have also gone beyond simply consuming media. By giving their petitions an online presence, students have become producers of digital content—using digital platforms for taking action on civic issues.

Making the Pitch
#elevatorspeech #signmypetition

Civic engagement also involves talking to people in person. Picture the man or woman with the clipboard in front of the grocery store, making a quick pitch and asking for a signature. Colley has something like this in mind when he requires students to write an "elevator pitch" (a 30-second pitch that explains what they are asking for and why they want someone to sign). The idea is to get a message across in the time it would take to go up or down an elevator. The pitch doesn't have to be catchy or clever, but it does need to be persuasive in a hurry. Students practice delivering their pitch in whatever public space they choose. Colley jokes that he doesn't really know whether or not students actually make the pitch. "At least they have an alternative to saying, 'Please sign this petition. It's for my class.'"

The elevator pitch and the petition are new genres for students. They call for language that will catch people's attention. Writers must make a fast, tight case that will get a message across, whether or not someone signs the petition. Colley believes these genres are worth learning. "Students are forced to justify their requests. It's about more than getting signatures."

The Call for Action
#thedemand #thejustification

When writers want readers to take some kind of action, they need to be specific in their appeal. "The demand is key," Colley explains. "You don't want your presentation to be just some kind of informative lecture. The demand can be 'Let's boycott.' And then you explain why that tactic will work."

To help students learn how to make a demand—or what Colley calls an "ask"—he has each group share its action plan, including the demand and justification, and get feedback from class members. He describes this process as a nerve-wracking time for students as they realize where the holes are in their attempts to persuade. "They want to be convincing," Colley says. "A lot of class assignments are directed to the teacher and they're about persuading the teacher, but I'm just one person, so there's not a lot of power to be gained in persuading me. . . . They already know how I feel about something."

Peer-to-peer response also provides added incentive to revise. Colley notes that the point of getting students to try out their plans with one another is to jump-start the rethinking they will need to do to make their voices heard.

PUTTING CIVIC ENGAGEMENT PROJECTS IN PERSPECTIVE

At this point, let's look at managing the scope of a long-term effort like Colley's civic engagement project, one that might seem daunting, even a bit surreal. In a follow-up report on the Educating for Democracy in a Digital Age (EDDA) initiative, Ellen Middaugh (2015) comments on a one-step-at-a-time approach:

> In the EDDA initiative, teachers are encouraged to think of civic action on a spectrum, considering how they can connect students to the community in small and large ways. For example, at the end of a research project, rather than having students simply write a paper to share with the teacher to be graded, students are asked to share the information they learned with a broader audience (through presentations, social media, posters, blogs, etc.). (pp. 5–6)

The idea for easing into a civic action project—perhaps starting with expanding audiences—might be just the right ticket for teachers who are new to the idea. Teachers who participated in the EDDA initiative used social media as a way for students to reach audiences outside the classroom—for example, Twitter, YouTube, Facebook, and YouthVoices.net.

> Teachers and students noted that having an authentic audience and getting comments from people they did not know was highly motivating. (Middaugh, 2015, p. 8)

In the written reflections and interviews that follow, two of Colley's students discuss the extent to which they learned what it takes to participate in a democracy, the potential impact of their work on an audience, and the ways they view their newfound roles as agents of change.

STUDENT REFLECTIONS
#insights #thinkingaboutthinking

Investigating and calling for action. These are make-or-break skills for Colley's 9th-graders. How important are they to any civic action? In an informal talk to local subscribers, *San Francisco Chronicle* editor Audrey Cooper emphasized the importance of investigating and calling for action in the newspaper. "Our job," she said, "is to shake the city by the shoulders and say 'wake up.' There's a problem here and then we need to point out ways to solve it" (personal communication, August 2, 2016).

Whether someone is a professional reporter or a first-year high school student, having the ability to rouse an audience, present evidence, and call for or propose solutions is pivotal to making a "wake up" call. The following post-project reflections reveal that Colley's 9th-graders learned about the skills and habits of mind required to engage in civic reform. After their experience participating in this project, many students wrote about the need to be persistent because of all the unexpected impediments along the way. They mentioned confidence (Mojo) as being key to convincing people who know little about an issue. Caring about their topic also made a difference, they said, when it came to talking to their audience.

A few students advocated for a bottom-up approach to change. One of those students was Megan Ma:

One lesson I will take away from my action project that I can use in the future to make positive change in the community is that it is not always best to target the top, most powerful people to accomplish change, and it can work just as well, or better, to work to create change with the help of the majority. We found that we would not create a lot of change by going through Tech's administration, and the best way to accomplish change was by going through the student body. I can apply this same idea if I wanted to make a change in anything else, like the city government. Rather than asking the mayor to make change, it would be more effective to tell fellow citizens about this positive change and all work together to ask our city's government to do something, as they are more likely to listen to a lot of people saying the same thing than one person.

In addition to learning about the dynamics of change as Megan did, students might also trade in some of their biases or stereotypes. Miles Chen, for example, worked on a project with four of his peers aimed at convincing the district to hire more translators for Asian parents. As part of the investigation, Miles concluded that many Asian American students who are not succeeding would be helped if parent–school communication were improved. Along the way, he discovered some of his own misperceptions and overgeneralizations:

In doing this project I learned a lot about myself. I learned that I have a very mainstream American view on Asians of all ethnicities. I realized that I too have the perception that all Asians succeed in school. Throughout the research phase of the project, I was astounded by the statistics we found on Southeast Asian high school and college graduation rates. I think that being an Asian American with good grades causes me to be biased in thinking that nobody with a similar identity to me could ever have a [problematic] background or ability.

In a sense, both Megan and Miles are reflecting on changes in their thinking. In Megan's case, she discovered the power of going to the people, while Miles reshaped, to some extent, his view of Asian Americans. *Writing to make an impact* is also about shifting attitudes for the writer, tipping the balance in favor of a new perspective.

When students try their hand at creating some kind of awareness or positive change, there's a lot of personal learning going on. Along with their individual revelations, they find out—sometimes to their dismay—how tricky it can be to work as a team. In this project, students worked with others who shared a common interest. We sat down with four them at the end of their civic action journey and asked them, "How did it go?"

HIGHS AND LOWS OF CIVIC ENGAGEMENT PROJECTS
#studentsweighin

Julia Batkhu, chief worrier and self-appointed monitor-of-progress of her civic engagement group, kept a watchful eye on assignments and deadlines. It wasn't always easy. "I worry a lot. I stress a lot. This is, like, a group project so it affects all of our grades." (All focus group quotes are from an interview, August 22, 2018.)

Julia and classmates Chosang Tenzin, Roboam Lopez, and Maxwell Hinkley agreed on the topic of disability rights. Each had a personal reason. Julia, for instance, went to a middle school "where a lot of disabled were treated differently." On one occasion, she witnessed a student having a seizure. Maxwell had several family members with disabilities. However, while the topic spoke to everyone in the group, their work together nevertheless began with tensions and disagreements.

First, and no surprise, not everyone felt the same urgency that Julia did about the schedule. In fact, it would be fair to say that there was a chasm between the way Julia, the worrier, worked, and the way Roboam approached his part of the project. "At one point," Julia described, "I looked over at the computer and he had two sentences done the day before it was due." While he admitted to being "the procrastinator," the one who drove Julia crazy, Roboam said he would never let the group down: "I always get it done at the last minute."

But the challenges went beyond work styles. During their initial conversations, no one could agree on a definition of *disabled*. "We had lots of arguments," Julia said. "We were at each other's throats. But even though there were conflicts, the conversations really helped." In the end, they agreed that *disabled* meant "any mental or physical disability that limits you from learning, speaking, or interacting."

As the project progressed, group members gathered and shared information via Google Docs, which brought a certain comfort to Julia: "We could see what everyone wrote and check the sources we used. We found a lot of primary sources like what special ed teachers thought about the topic. That helped us out a lot."

After reading about the views of special education teachers, the foursome wanted to interview someone on their own campus. However, finding and scheduling a teacher interview proved difficult and they had to rely on Colley to make the contact.

The interview proved valuable because it opened up new insights and questions. "We felt like we were getting the inside story. We learned that mainstream teachers often don't get very much help working with disabled students, and when they do, it's limited."

Chosang, in particular, zeroed in on the fact that many efforts to help the disabled target physical barriers—for example, the need for ramps. But what about learning disabilities? Couldn't teachers benefit if the school provided more comprehensive information/training on how to support special-needs students academically?

And then the group uncovered another issue: isolation. Too often, disabled students lived somewhere in a dark corner of the campus. When they showed up in a real-life setting, they were vulnerable. Julia watched one disabled student struggle to make himself understood while other students mocked him:

Across from one of my classes there's a Burger King. A student was there to order a cheeseburger but he couldn't physically say it. Other kids were making fun of him, making hand gestures and stuttering, and, like, laughing about it. Ever since I started the Take Action Project, I am more sensitive about the topic, how much disabilities really affect and isolate students. It angers me that students make jokes about it.

A Big Win
#socialmediabonus

For all their growing awareness, Julia, Roboam, Chosang, and Maxwell were still 9th-graders with a healthy sense of competition. The highlight of their project was almost accidental. Chosang put the petition for more teacher training on her Instagram. An enterprising friend shared the link and the signatures started rolling in. Every 24 hours, the number bumped up, from 100 to 500 to more than 1,000. According to Maxwell, their classmates were blown away: "It got announced in class. Everyone went crazy. Oh, can you give us some of your signatures?"

Clearly, the four were dizzy with their unexpected triumph. "We're at the bottom of the totem pole," Roboam said, "but this 1,000 signatures shows how much support we have." Julia agreed: "We don't have enough power to make someone do something, but we have enough power to bring the issue up. "

However, as it turned out, their power to close the deal fell short.

A Typical Roadblock
#theshutout

The last step in the civic action project never happened. According to Maxwell, "Our plan was to go talk to the principal and to say 'look at all the supporters we have.'" All four students acknowledged the principal was really busy: "We emailed her and she didn't respond. We went to the office and a coworker said she was in a meeting." Plan B was to talk to a vice principal. But how to get an appointment?

In our conversations with students over several years, we have heard stories like this before. Students expect an immediate answer to a letter or email and come away disappointed when they strike out. On one hand, this is a reality. Not everyone can accommodate time-consuming requests or interactions with students. On the other hand, Roboam is right. Students are at the bottom of the totem pole in situations like these. They aren't hooked up with those in authority, and they don't necessarily know how to get access or attention. Learning the ropes when it comes to contacting higher ups—including the disappointments—is part of the package.

The Takeaways
#thingstoremember

 Going to the top has no guarantees. Much as we want kids to make significant connections with people in the school and the community, for all of the reasons above, they may run into a few roadblocks. Sometimes it pays off to help students make a contact or get an interview, as Colley chose to do. But talk about busy people! Teachers can't do it all. Some teachers like Laury Fischer have students in the class help one another find resources.

 Clarifying expectations is probably a good thing. Not everyone is going to welcome an invitation to talk to students. The further up the food chain, the less likely "important" people might make themselves available—not that students shouldn't try. But learning to entertain alternatives makes sense. When the principal isn't available, how about the vice principal or counselor or coach or teacher or custodian—someone who knows a lot but doesn't necessarily sit in the big office?

> You may never know what results come from your action. But if you do nothing there will be no result.
> —Mahatma Gandhi

 Solving the problem is not the measure of success. A successful project has these elements: selecting a real topic or issue, conducting research, working productively in a team, communicating ideas and findings to others, *writing to make an impact*, and learning from the experience.

MOTIVATING STUDENTS TO TAKE ACTION
#lightingthefire

In our investigation into civic action and what makes it compelling, we visited another high school to talk to a group of 17- and 18-year-olds and their teacher, Judy Kennedy, about what features of a civic action project energize them.

How the Project Worked
#planofaction

To take on their chosen topic—gun violence—Jonathan Sira, Andres Robles, Sal Escalera, and Jaqueline Gonzalez proposed raising the age for owning a gun while exploring what they could do to make things safer in their own community. During the 8 weeks of the project, they worked through a number of action steps, including the following:

- Conducting a survey among their peers to gauge the extent to which others agreed on the seriousness of gun violence
- Interviewing a police officer who emphasized "speaking up"
- Circulating a petition around campus
- Conducting research on recent episodes of gun violence, looking for common threads
- Presenting their work to their peers

Civic Action and Life Stories
#directconnections

Ask students about a long-term school project and you can count on at least one response. Guaranteed. "There wasn't enough time," somebody will complain, and everyone else will solemnly agree. We expected to hear the age-old lament when we interviewed Jonathan, Andres, Sal, and Jaqueline about their civic action project, an assignment for their senior government class. And we did. Learning to manage time is part of every challenging project, both in and out of school. But we also heard how each of their individual narratives elevated the project for them. (All focus group quotes are from an interview, January 17, 2019.)

We began by watching a class presentation by the four students, who described their collaborative research and action steps to address the issue of gun violence. Something that stood out for us was the personal and pressing nature of their topic. At one time, each had lost a friend or family member in their own community. They also experienced a nagging shared worry— the presence of gun violence in their daily lives. "My parents won't let me go just anywhere with my friends," Jonathan told us. Jaqueline mentioned a recent robbery at a nearby store in the mall where she works. "We are emotionally attached to the subject because our neighborhoods are not that safe," Jonathan explained.

After the presentation, we sat down with these students—and later with their teacher, Judy Kennedy—to explore further the way past and current life circumstances affect their work in school. We learned that they had few opportunities in their high school careers to pick their own topics. All four students insisted that being able to choose the focus for their project was key to the whole enterprise, along with the go-ahead to select their team members.

Kennedy agreed:

The whole buy-in is having a choice of topics and teammates. I tell students to find people they trust who have shared experiences, who they can count on, and who they enjoy talking to. They have to be in touch with each other outside of class, so they need to find teammates they can rely on, who will answer their texts, who will get together maybe even on vacations. (All Kennedy quotes in this chapter are from a personal communication, July 20, 2018.)

Jonathan explained how he decided whom to work with on the project. His comment illustrates one way students interpreted Kennedy's guidelines:

> I've known Andres since 1st grade and he's always been my boy. Obviously, we were going to be together and choose each other. I've played baseball with Sal through my whole life. I know these people so they're going to have my back. When we were picking groups, I wanted to have people who I knew I could rely on through this whole project. (All focus group comments are from an interview, February 26, 2018.)

Life Stories and Getting the Job Done
#findingcommonground

The most challenging part of the project was getting the job done outside of class. Again, Jonathan explained his dilemma:

> After school, I go to baseball practice and then to work and by then I want to go to bed. [To communicate with one another] we had a group text. You would send something. One person might send something back. It just depended. All of us were at work and sometimes you wouldn't get a response until 12 midnight. We never seemed to be doing the same thing at the same time.

Kennedy found Jonathan's comments "really representative:"

> The stress level is high when students have to depend on each other. What happens when a kid doesn't pull his or her weight and messes up the team? A project like this takes stamina and perseverance and good communication. These are other reasons why it's important that students care about their topic and their teammates.
>   [These students] were enthusiastic about the project and about working together. They were not the class valedictorians and they were not on the same place on the political spectrum. But they found common ground on something that was bothering them. In terms of enthusiasm and taking a project seriously, these four students were at the top of the class.

During our hour-long conversation with the students, we picked up on their enthusiasm and gritty commitment to getting the job done. Though we didn't hear the word *fun*, the students talked positively about feeling accomplished and also satisfied because they had spoken up about an issue that affected their lives.

When students have a lot of choice, it also can pay off for the teacher, according to Kennedy: "I like it so much when kids pick something important to them. I learn a ton. I have adult conversations with the students. We bounce ideas off each other. I learn what the kids learn."

In the long run, how much will students remember about what they learned from their research? What do we remember about our assigned research papers in high school? Not much. But students who participate in a project where the writing and speaking makes something happen will no doubt remember, if not all of the substance, at least the experience of being civically engaged. "We're just kids from down the street in our community," Jonathan told us. "I believe that even the smallest voices can make the biggest impact."

> Ultimately, students get something they might not have expected—a whiff of power.

The Takeaways
#thingstoremember

 Projects like this one shift the responsibility and ownership to the students. The more choices they have concerning topic and team, the more committed they are likely to be to the purpose. Need we add that this will not be neat and tidy?

 The process of completing a long-term project does not have to be a death march, but having a tight, well-defined timeline with deadlines and checkpoints helps students organize their time.

 Allocating some class time for students to work together takes some of the pressure off.

TEACHING PLAYBOOK

Finding the Story Behind the Topic
#itspersonal

Personal experience is a starting point for selecting a topic, according to Stan Pesick: "It's important that students care about the subject, that they understand what's at stake and why. How do they know an issue is worth investigating? What's their connection to it? Our values underlie the way we see the world" (personal communication, November 20, 2017).

To find the story behind the topic, Judy Kennedy asks her students to write a short piece (a paragraph or two), making a case for the topic they chose for their civic action project before embarking on the research. Here's where the power of personal narrative as a starting point really shows up. Note that in each of the examples below, some life event or memory or condition has set the direction for the topic the students chose:

- Train track safety: To prevent future deaths, one of Kennedy's students wanted to highlight the danger of walking or playing on train tracks after a close friend was struck and killed by an Amtrak train. By taking action in this way, the student also felt she could make a tribute to her friend.
- Teen depression and suicide: Citing her own experiences with depression, one student wanted to advocate for help for teenagers, particularly in a climate where more of them are suffering from this disorder.
- Rehabilitating the Hayward shoreline: Citing the memory of birding, fishing, and walking along the shoreline with his grandparents, another student argued that it should again be a peaceful place to go and experience nature.

Gathering Resources for a Chosen Topic
#wheretogo #whototalkto

It's one thing to come up with a topic. It's another entirely to know what to do next and where to find good information. We talked to one of our Writing Project colleagues about how to jump-start and maintain all the resources a writer needs for a big project.

Laury Fischer helps his students discover multiple resources and word-of-mouth recommendations. Before any writing occurs, each student writes down his/her chosen topic on a piece of paper. The papers then circulate throughout the class, where other students jot down suggestions about what to read, who to talk to, where to visit, and so on. Fischer emphasizes the need for interview contacts because "that's where people are usually shy and need an 'oh, my uncle is a social worker—you can talk to him' kind of thing'" (personal communication, June 12, 2014).

Fischer also encourages students to use emails, texts, and tweets so they can communicate outside of class to let one another know when they come across something on TV or someone interesting to interview. In other words, Fischer guides his students to do what anyone would do in the face of a question or a project: Ask someone who may have some tips. Trade information. Keep one another posted.

Managing Long-term Projects
#dealingwithdeadlines #managingtime

Does this sound familiar?

> Chances are you've seen this scenario before. You give your students three weeks
> to work on a collaborative project. You start out with total buy-in. They're excited
> about what they will create. But a week later, you run into issues. Students aren't
> making any progress. One group has barely even started. Another has had fifteen
> false starts and they keep changing what they are making. (Spencer, 2018, para. 1)

This scenario explains what comes next: a list of suggestions from some of
our favorite teachers about helping students learn project management:

- 👍 Break the project into manageable chunks, and give each one a
  deadline date.
- 👍 Give students time in their groups to define their chosen issue, make
  goals, divide up tasks, and plan a way to share their work outside
  of class (such as Google Docs). Recall that Colley's student Julia
  described her team's beginning debate as essential to their process.
- 👍 Post a list of the deliverables on the whiteboard: what and when
  things are due, along with models fastened on the board with
  magnetic clips. Judy Kennedy invites students to come in any time
  to read the samples.
- 👍 Offer and model different planning strategies for students to manage
  their out-of-school time: checklists, to-do lists, Post-its, personal or
  group calendars, notes on smartphones, group member emails and
  texts, plus text/email self-reminders.
- 👍 Schedule periodic 10-minute check-ins for group members at the
  beginning of class. Judy Kennedy posts goals on the board for these
  quick strategy sessions.
- 👍 Set a "pre-deadline" for each task—2 days or so ahead of the posted
  deadline—when students can bring their penultimate drafts for
  teacher help.

Opening Up Possibilities for Writing
#openfieldrunning #notetakingnotemaking

Civic action projects can accommodate all kinds of writing, from note-taking
to public speeches. We have looked closely at petitions and elevator pitches as
genres that take some front-loading because they are new for most students.
There are, of course, many other options, depending on how teachers design
(or taper into) their projects:

- Blogs
- Digital stories
- Documentaries/mockumentaries
- Final reports
- Journalistic stories/articles
- Letters to elected officials or other authorities
- Narrative/poetry/hip-hop with social purpose
- Op-eds
- Podcasts
- PowerPoints
- Prezis
- Speeches
- Public service announcements (PSA)
- Multimedia presentations
- Videos

In addition to the flashier options for polished products like these, civic action projects include all kinds of process-oriented writing tasks that don't have to be graded:

- Email requests for interviews and/or information
- Goal-setting and planning notes
- To-do lists, calendars, texts, and emails among group members
- Early drafts
- Interview and survey questions
- Scripts and storyboards
- Reflections
- Note-taking/note-making

Of all of these possibilities, note-taking/note-making deserves special mention because it takes students beyond simply recording information from their research. Note-taking is exactly what you would expect: dutifully transcribing facts, data, ideas, and so on. Note-making, on the other hand, is the process the writer uses to make sense of the notes. This might include, for example, the following:

- Asking questions
- Making connections to other sources or to personal experience
- Analyzing
- Noting chunks of information to be included in the student's report or presentation
- Identifying gaps in information

In short, note-making is the personal commentary on the notes. Teachers who have used this technique have often asked students to take their notes in the left-hand column of a paper or screen and make their corresponding comments in the right-hand column.

Science teacher Bob Tierney introduced this strategy to Bay Area Writing Project teachers with the idea that they could use it in any discipline. According to Tierney, the strategy works for reading, research, and lectures, or for any time students need to process information.

Writing Project teacher Susan Reed (1988) developed a variation called the WOW log. In this instance, students select and record various quotes from their reading and explain why the quote merits a "wow." When students need to embed quotations, expert opinions, or evidence in their writing, their WOW log serves as an effective starter kit.

In the next chapter, we take up using writing to learn, understand, and figure things out. Both the note-making and the WOW log are handy tools in these situations.

Resources for Civic Engagement Writing

For more information about and examples of civic engagement projects, try one or two of the resources below:

- www.teachingchannel.org/video/prepare-civic-engagement-edda
- www.crfcap.org
- Steven Zemelman, *From Inquiry to Action: Civic Engagement with Project-Based Learning in All Content Areas* (2016)
- www.edutopia.org/discussion/14-examples-high-quality-civic-learning-opportunities
- www.carnegie.org/media/filer_public/ab/dd/abdda62e-6e84-47a4-a043-348d2f2085ae/ccny_grantee_2011_guardian.pdf
- Steven Zemelman, "Guest Post/Ideas for Student Civic Action in a Time of Social Uncertainty," *New York Times*, May 18, 2017. Retrieved from www.nytimes.com/2017/05/18/learning/lesson-plans/guest-post-ideas-for-student-civic-action-in-a-time-of-social-uncertainty.html
- www.crf-usa.org/online-lessons-index/free-lessons-index.html

CHAPTER 6

Writing to Figure Things Out

For those of us who occasionally (or frequently) slouch on the couch to watch some sporting event, picture those sweaty athletes between games, hunched over a journal, log, or notebook. In his article "Learning from Athletes: Creating Activity Journals," teacher and soccer coach Rich Kent (2014) describes what goes on when his soccer players reflect on and evaluate their performances and set goals for what they need to do next:

> Their writing is authentic and at times gritty; most of my players are all in because they're doing real work that matters to them. It's exactly what we want from the students in our classrooms. Even the sweat. (p. 68)

Kent attributes his interest in using journals with both students and athletes to James Atwater, whose words Kent scribbled down in his own journal:

> Expressive writing enables [students] to make sense for themselves of what they have seen or read or done or talked about by composing it for themselves in their own words. Thus expressive writing is fundamental to learning—in any subject matter—because it enables [students] to internalize knowledge, to make it part of themselves, by putting it together in their own terms. (Atwater, 1981, p. 4, as cited in Kent, 2014, p. 71)

Lest this kind of writing seem hopelessly past tense—like some kind of English teacher throwback to an earlier, warm and fuzzy era—Kent identifies a number of 21st-century athletes who rely on writing in training logs, journals, or team notebooks to inform their practice, adjust their attitudes, or preserve their memories, including tennis star Serena Williams, Olympic swimmer Michael Phelps, ski sensation Lindsey Vonn, baseball player Carlos Delgado, and golfer Johnson Wagner. From where we stand, athletes like these are *writing to make an impact* on themselves, with the goal of improving their performance.

Like Kent, many teachers have routinely invited students to reflect on their learning or their processes or something important that has happened in their lives—on the field or off. Reflective writing is a wide-open genre, unfenced and, in some ways, underexplored. Exactly what kinds of things happen when students have the chance to think back in writing about some task or challenge?

ABOUT THIS CHAPTER:
REFLECTIVE WRITING TO ENHANCE LEARNING

In the previous chapter, we looked at some reflective writing from Matt Colley's class, along with reflective conversations from two different groups of students about their experiences with their civic action projects. In this chapter, we explore four classroom situations in which students reflect about their learning in a specific discipline:

1. A high school economics class: 12th-graders write both ongoing and final reflections about the choices they make in a project called "How to Make a Living."
2. A high school science class: Biology students participate in a homegrown experiment to find out if writing about their learning makes any difference when it comes to their ultimate success at test time.
3. Another high school science class: Students keep ongoing journals about their learning and, with their teacher's encouragement, their questions and curiosities.
4. A high school social studies class: Students check in on Google Forms, noting their progress and challenges, as a way to keep their teacher up to date and able to give them useful, on-the-spot help.

Because these classes focused on content in a particular subject area, the reflective writing students did was designed to make an impact on their learning in a discipline—for instance, thinking critically, exploring ideas, managing processes, making connections, boosting achievement, assessing quality of the work, providing information to the teacher, and solidifying strengths and abilities for the students. That's a lot to ask of writing, for sure.

Reflective writing, then, enhances the quality of students' learning and also helps them learn on their own. In *How People Learn: Brain, Mind, Experience, and School*, the authors say that teachers should incorporate metacognitive skills in all subject areas, to "enhance student achievement and develop in students the ability to learn independently" (National Research Council, 2000, p. 21). While they recognize the need for students to learn the content of a discipline, they also point out that realistically, there is way too much content for students—or, for that matter, scholars—to master, no matter how dedicated they are or how long they live. The key is to give students opportunities to understand and make sense of topics so they can continue fruitful explorations on their own wherever they are as a learner.

Our examples, plus the teaching playbook, provide some ways to tailor reflective writing when the goal is to broaden and deepen learning.

CLASSROOM CLOSEUP:
MAKING ECONOMICS PERSONALLY MEANINGFUL
#makealiving

High school social studies teacher Judy Kennedy reels in her second-semester seniors—often (mentally) well on their way out the school door—with a project called "How to Make a Living" (HTML). Each week, these 17- and 18-year-olds make a virtual decision about an aspect of living on their own based on the information they gather during the project. They begin by scouring the Internet for a job, one that doesn't require a college degree, since they are not yet college graduates. Then the fun begins. They go on to make decision after decision—for example:

- Find and furnish an apartment
- Choose a mode of transportation to get to work
- Pick a utilities package
- Set aside money for food, general living expenses, and entertainment

The goal of the project is to learn how to live within your means. The project includes mini-lessons like these:

- Buying car insurance
- Selecting a health care plan
- Writing checks
- Choosing a credit card
- Paying taxes
- Setting up retirement programs

With these mini-lessons, students do more than listen to the teacher. For example, they actually find a health care plan that fits their needs, and though they don't plunk down any real money, they do make a specific choice.

Twice during the project, *life happens*. Kennedy has the students draw slips of paper that describe unexpected events and expenses—for instance, a speeding or parking ticket, car breakdown, stolen cellphone, or permanently misplaced keys. One or two coveted slips offer some good news like a bonus. Toward the end of the project, the *life-happens* events become more serious. Students draw slips that say they have lost their jobs, broken their legs, become parents, and so on. Occasionally, a student draws a job promotion. Kennedy reports "much pandemonium" in the classroom.

All along the way, students have to keep a 6-month budget. They also have to account in writing for every decision they make. Why this job? Why this furniture? Why this much money for going out on a Saturday night? There is no penalty for making a "wrong" decision, or for putting a "want" ahead of a "need." The whole point is to learn about decisions that will keep students out of debt. At the end of the project, students engage in a longer piece of writing in which they revisit and reflect on their individual experiences.

Student Writing

When you read these excerpts from the students' final reflections, think about what's happening for the writer—both in new understandings about managing money and also in changed attitudes or perceptions. After all, how many teenagers come equipped with financial savvy? The writing is one clue to what and how much they've figured out.

Budget Wisdom Gained in a High School Economics Class
By Homero Alejo

I think that the "Life Happens" [assignment] shows my best effort because it not only requires me to be realistic but also creative. This assignment made me be realistic in the way that life really hits you with unexpected turns. In this assignment my scenario was being laid off. This is always a possibility in the workplace without a union. It's a realistic scenario that not everyone is prepared for. I took this scenario seriously and asked myself what it is that I would really do in this situation. I considered my options and it definitely forced me to make changes in my monthly budget. . . . My solution to being laid off was a mobile service of car maintenance on the Taskrabbit app where I performed maintenance on cars for a lower price than the competition with the same quality in service. This ends up getting lots of customers which helps me stay on my feet while being laid off.

In this reflection, Homero assesses the amount of thought he put into one of the weekly assignments and explains why this particular assignment captured his imagination. He articulates a process for solving a real-life problem: Ask yourself questions, look at options, change your spending plan, and find a temporary solution to stay on your feet.

How Making A Living Sucks (If you don't know what you're doing)
By Luz Munoz

The other mini project that I learned from is the credit card interview because I had to actually contact someone to tell me their story in credit cards. To be honest I was already scared about credit cards and now that I have actually learned about them and discussed about them with someone older it made me more scared. I am terrified of going into debt. What I learned however is that if you stay on top of your payment and don't exceed your limit, you will be fine but if you miss just one payment interest can go out the roof and it will be very hard to get back on track. Moral of the story, don't forget to pay!

Luz has the right idea, for sure. She's ready for "real life," at least as far as making credit card payments on time. But on another level, she has also figured out, in the best of circumstances, how a person gets some control over debt, and that's a leap that many adults have yet to make.

In the next excerpt, note that this 18-year-old writer uses her own discoveries during the How to Make a Living Project to empathize with others who get by day to day with meager resources. She comes to understand what she will need to do to make a better living when she is out in the world.

Well I Sure Hope It Doesn't Turn Out Like This
By Debbie Mendez

From this overall project I was forced to see just how hard it is to live while making minimum wage. You like to believe they'll be some left over at the end of each month, and that you'll work with that, but no a lot of the times that isn't the case, which as stated before, sucks! It actually kind of makes me want to cry, thinking of people who have to feed families off of minimum wage, and have to resort to bad eating habits, and lack of certain things in order to make it. It also reassured me that, working at a low paying job, because I can't get a higher one, due to my lack of education in this assignment, is not a path I want to go down. I realize I'll have to get a starter job even with a college degree, but still it'll be better than $10.50 an hour. I honestly applaud the people that live off of these types of payments, because it is way to easy to lose money. Overall the project just reminds me of the importance of an education, responsibility, and budgeting!

We asked our colleague Mark St. John, president of Inverness Research Inc., to comment on what happens in this writing. He notes that the student's thinking, appreciation, knowledge, and awareness are growing: "By writing about it, it makes it real for . . . [the student], as well as perhaps for others." St. John also notes that in this kind of writing, students "crystallize" parts of their experience: "They are writing to make something happen for themselves" (personal communication, June 30, 2017).

In this next excerpt, Tiara Brown nails the essential question when it comes to spending: What do I really need? Her title also captures what she thinks about the project she just completed. She has dipped into adulthood (separate from her current "real life"), and she's tried to toe the line in the face of temptation.

The Adult Experience
By Tiara Brown

While making some of my decisions I was thinking "Do I REALLY need this?" and "Is it on sale?" and even "Where can I get this for cheaper price?" Doing this project I was thinking that I don't even see how most adults are surviving without pulling their hair out. . . . Doing this project I strictly told myself that I would purchase things only that I NEEDED. And if I were to have some extra money I can treat myself. Nothing too fancy though. I wanted to purchase an iPhone (yes in real life too) but I wasn't going to spend $300+ on a phone when I already have one and it's only $67. Making decisions that benefit me are easy but not when you feel like buying an expensive bag or in my case an expensive meal.

Our final excerpt illustrates one of the high points in learning: "I learned who I am. . . ." It also represents *writing to make an impact* on the writer. Notice how many things Merissa takes away from the project.

Conclusions and Uncovering Monetary Delusions
By Merissa Amador

There are a lot of things I learned from this project but mostly I learned who I am financially, not a risk taker. I learned that I like stability, a lot of it. . . . I also learned a numerous amount of tips and little do's and don'ts, like don't get a credit card if I know I won't have a stable enough amount of money where I can pay way more than the minimum each month. Do save, all the time, that's a big one and while I didn't just learn it I learned to really appreciate the importance of it. The last and biggest thing I learned is expect anything, life happens and while it is unpredictable when it will happen I can always prepare so that when it does finally happen I'm not on top of an antenna tower waiting for the lightning to strike.

In all of the excerpts, Kennedy's students analyze what has happened during the project. The student writers figure out their personal takeaways. They also figure out where they fit in the big world of making a living, what their standards are, and how they make choices.

What Students Learn from Reflecting
#boostingcontent #bringingithome

For teacher Judy Kennedy, her students' reflections confirm her belief in the value of doing metacognitive thinking in writing: "The more my students think on paper, the more they think about their financial choices and why they made them. They are learning about themselves as they become financially literate. Without the writing, they would just be doing an assignment" (personal communication, July 30, 2018).

Kennedy notes that her students "love the project because it's really relevant for them. They see the real life behind their choices of things like buying a car. The majority of their learning is in the reflections, their explanations of why they bought that car when they had so many other choices."

Kennedy never grades down when students go into debt: "I'm looking for them to inform themselves." Kennedy also appreciates what happens between parents and teenagers as the project progresses. "You can see it in the reflec-

> The more my students think on paper, the more they think about their financial choices and why they made them.
> —Judy Kennedy

tions. Kids often write about how grateful they are to their parents. They come to understand what their parents have sacrificed."

Along the way, Kennedy, too, learns from her students' reflections—for example, "if the lessons are effective, if the takeaways are what I wanted, or if I pushed them hard enough."

Reflective writing, then, makes things happen for the writer *and* for the teacher. Bill Rice, CEO/founder of Kaleidico, a digital marketing agency, advocates for this kind of writing precisely because it gives both writers and readers new insights:

> Many people believe that the only reason to write is to demonstrate your cleverness or authority on a topic. I personally find writing much more valuable as a means to think, to learn, and ultimately to understand. Unsurprisingly, I find this kind of writing also the most interesting to read. Nothing is more engaging than reading the thoughts of a true novice seeking their way through a new endeavor. (Rice, 2013)

FIGURING THINGS OUT THROUGH WRITING IN THE DISCIPLINES
#writingasinquiry #writingtoremember

A classic study on writing in science influenced a generation or more of subject-area teachers and maintains its relevance today. Bob Tierney (1981), a California biology teacher, decided to test out a theory he had after participating in the Bay Area Writing Project summer institute. Together with a colleague, Harry Stookey, Tierney created an experimental and comparison group among 136 biology students. Both groups studied the same topics at the same time with the same labs and homework assignments. But the experimental group (which switched between teachers at the semester to negate the "teacher variable") received an array of writing assignments, including reading logs, "neuron notes" (learning logs), group writing, and lab reports to audiences outside the classroom.

When it came to the moment of truth, however, the multiple-choice unit tests showed no significant difference between the two groups, much to Tierney's dismay. However, on the recall tests—given 16 weeks after the fall genetics unit and 3 weeks after the spring seed-plants unit—the experimental group outscored the comparison group. According to Tierney and Stookey, the students who had the chance to use expressive writing to learn and understand the subject matter more completely also retained more of their learning (National Writing Project & Nagin, 2006).

Across the country, a young science teacher, John Dorroh (1993), followed the work of his colleague Tierney. Dorroh, who attended the Writing Project in south Mississippi, invented the Expressive Mode journal for his science students to mull over what they were learning. "As often as possible," Dorroh wrote with them during the 6 or 7 minutes of writing time. That's how he discovered for himself the value of expressive writing—writing to learn and figure things out. "I surprise myself," he explained, "with words and thoughts and questions" (p. 28):

> Virus. The very word frightens me. It's not a living thing but can and does appear to be so, at least within the confines of a healthy, living cell. A singular invasion, one nasty particle, stripping itself of its protein coat, 'knowing' telepathically that something delicious lies inside this innocent cell. Massive annihilation, total destruction leaving a disease-stricken body. Life or death?
>
> Will it be the flu, a terrible, annoying cold, chicken pox, or AIDS? Will it attack someone famous, or someone simple like me? Will it be an Austrian, a banker, an entertainer? Will it result in death? How many days of work or school will its victim miss?
>
> What is the origin of this non-living, super-destructive particle? What is its biological niche? Did it evolve for the sole purpose of suppressing healthy tissue? And where will it end? Will viruses be the ultimate conquerors of our planet? Inquiring minds want to know. (1993, pp. 28–29)

When Dorroh (1993) read this piece to his class, one student immediately asked if he already knew the answers to all the questions he asked. "I sure don't. Writing freely about viruses made me think hard about them. . . ." (p. 29).

Students don't always pick up on the fact that scientists ask lots of questions—that they are always exploring "why." Anson and Beach (1995) recommend an approach like Dorroh's:

> [Students] have not yet acquired the specific thought processes associated with what it means to be a historian, scientist, mathematician or translator. By using journals in different subject areas, students gain practice in thinking like historians, scientists, mathematicians or translators. (p. 52).

Whether it's in a journal, a team notebook, or a learning log, and regardless of subject area, teachers can use writing to help students think critically about content:

> Even more to the point, students can explore concepts, make connections, conceive ideas through writing if every piece of writing isn't supposed to be formal, complete, and correct, a caricature of what is published in academic journals. Write to learn! (Herman, 1989, p. 16)

While the heavy emphasis in much of the today's curricula—the incoming tide, so to speak—is on academic writing and source-based writing, expressive or reflective writing allows for a different kind of participation in the discipline: one that permits exploration, rethinking, flailing around, figuring things out, and finding out what you know and don't know. It involves the best kind of notes-to-self with reminders, observations, questions, aha moments, associations, parallels, appreciations—you get the idea. It's *writing to make an impact* when learning is the priority.

CLASSROOM CLOSEUP:
USING REFLECTIONS TO STOP AND TAKE STOCK
#Customizinginthemoment

Hillary Walker teaches history and English in grades 6–12 in a public high school in Oakland, California. In an endeavor to break things down for her 12th-graders, mostly English learners, she engages them in a series of exercises aimed at learning how to do research on the Internet and how to present that research to a peer audience.

Each week, Walker conducts a check-in with her students via a reflection in Google Forms:

> I collect information on how confident my students feel about conducting Internet research, what they are struggling with, which segment of the writing they are focusing on, something they learned. The reflections tell me where there are gaps and where to anticipate gaps in the future. I still have my general arc, but the reflections help me adapt and reemphasize. (All Walker quotes are from a personal communication, April 23, 2018.)

> The reflections tell me where there are gaps and where to anticipate gaps in the future.
> —Hillary Walker

Walker notes that she has always asked students for reflections at the end of projects, but could never use these final reflections strategically along the way. Now, when students mention problems and challenges, Walker offers individual writing conferences. But the entire class can benefit as well. "I do a lot more explicit teaching after I read the reflections."

Monitoring Progress
#weeklycheckin

The first thing you might note when you read the student comments below is their brevity. These are quick responses to whatever questions Walker poses, questions that change over time. Here are some examples:

- What is an interesting finding?
- How many citations does your annotated bibliography currently have?
- What do you need to be successful this week?

Take a look at these sample responses from different students for quick clues about their progress, attitudes, and needs:

What is something you're feeling proud of at this moment?

- I am on track and not procrastinating.
- I already interviewed 10 people.
- That I was able to talk about my work and explained pretty well in my opinion.
- The slides were pretty good, but I for sure am going to need help with my essay.
- Getting this over with.

What is a clear next step that you are already working on?

- I need to do more researching.
- Reading my books, which I forgot :(and pulling out quotes.
- Need to redo my findings and make it more clear.
- Starting my slides and finding images.

What kinds of feedback did you receive from your group [after the presentations]?

- To put less words in my slides.
- They told me to look at the audience.
- I have a strong topic.
- To finish up and be sure to include good evidence and background context.

- To work a little bit more on my evidence and to start interviewing others.
- My slides were well organized and I had a good idea of what I was doing.
- They weren't the best at giving me feedback.

Going to the Source
#askstudents

Walker's ongoing dialogue with her students about their work and learning—and the way she follows their lead with changes or tweaks in her teaching—makes sense. Patricia Fox (1998) believes that asking students directly about their progress is the way to go:

> If we want to know what students are thinking, what their intentions are and how well their work has measured up to their own standards, why guess? ... [A]s Kathleen Blake Yancey (1998) suggests in *Reflection in the Writing Classroom*, why not "try asking 'em'"? Yancey credits the early studies of the writing process by Sondra Perl and Janet Emig, among others with establishing the notion of "students as authoritative informants." (p. 37)

As a weekly practice, an exchange like Walker's with her students seems doable—a way to make something happen without a pile of papers to read. This is not in-depth reflection about what students have learned. Rather, it's a management tool, if you will, to monitor progress and identify next steps. It encourages students to take responsibility and ask for help, which, in turn, allows teachers to customize that help in the moment.

Writing About Writing
#makelearningvisible

So, where does reflection fit into a writing classroom? It was popular back in the 1980s and early 1990s, when portfolios were in vogue, for teachers to ask students to reflect on questions like these:

- How did you write this piece?
- What do you see as its special strengths?
- What part of the process was hardest for you? What was easiest?
- If you could go on working on this piece, what would you do?
- What have you learned about writing from your work?
- What is your next goal?

Researchers like Roberta Camp (1990), Paul LeMahieu et al. (1995), and Kathleen Yancey (1998), and teachers like Kathryn Howard (1990) and Patricia

Fox (1998) generated hundreds of reflective prompts, plus reasons for asking students to think about their writing and writing processes. But like many other innovative practices in education, this one fell off the radar in favor of more product-oriented approaches, spurred on by standardized assessments and movements like the Common Core.

> Robust reflection begins with the invention or planning stages of writing and continues during the writing itself, in addition to involving a looking back after the writing is completed, or at each completed draft.
> —Kara Taczak and Liane Robertson

So here's our 21st-century pitch: Just like learning content, learning to write is vast and, at times, unforgiving, especially for developing writers. Questions like those above remain useful. To the extent that young writers have nailed down some things they do well, or a process that works for them, their writing tasks—both present and future—will be easier. For example, if students figure out that making notes before writing is a useful technique, it's likely that strategy will be available to them whenever they sit down to write. Writing about strategies that work makes them "conscious and retrievable. . . . In this way, [students] can call on these strategies, draw from their personal bank account whenever they sit down to write. They no longer have to depend solely on some kind of happy accident to make their writing successful" (Smith, 1993, p. 6).

Further, when students learn to assess their own work, the quality of their writing improves. In their report *Informing Writing: The Benefits of Formative Assessment*, Graham, Harris, and Herbert (2011) write: "Self-evaluation of writing had a consistently positive impact on the quality of students' writing. These gains occurred for students in grades three to twelve" (pp. 18–19).

Writing to figure things out gives students a boost in self-knowledge, in acquiring knowledge, in recall, in discipline-based thinking, and in performance. It's a win, win, win—five times over.

TEACHING PLAYBOOK

Writing Afterwords
#moretosay

You've seen them at the end of books. Afterwords are often stories about how a book came into being or how the author discovered and developed the idea; they might also be closing comments from the author about the work itself. When authors write about their work (and themselves), they put their readers on the inside, giving them the story behind the story.

Like professional writers, student writers have reasons to write about their work. They are never short of opinions about the assignment or examples of how hard and long they worked. But more important, their stories solidify for *them* how they get their ideas or what they do when the paper or screen is blank. If they have a chance to share their afterwords, they can learn from their peers— for example, that ideas pop up during showers, or on long runs, or while doing the dishes, or in the middle of the night. For teachers, afterwords can be a gold-mine of clues about the context for a particular piece, about the challenges or tri-umphs the author encountered in creating it, and about successful (and maybe idiosyncratic) strategies the author might share with the whole class.

Start anywhere. Ask a simple question: "How did you write this piece?" and take it from there. The questions on p. 91 will also make good starting points. Consider commenting only on the afterword when you are buried in grading. That's where students have consolidated their learning and where you can usefully reinforce that learning.

Reflecting Together on Final Drafts
#recognizingefforts #celebratingaccomplishments

Does this typical farewell to final drafts look familiar? The teacher ruins his or her social life grading student writing and crafting laborious comments. The students read the grade and complain. They might skim the comments and, most likely, they will compare results (more complaining) before putting the paper to permanent rest.

Here are a few ideas for keeping that final draft alive where it can do some good and make a few things happen:

- Conduct a read-around of finished drafts or excerpts from drafts.
- Establish an author's chair or podium where students can read aloud. Be sure to talk about the strengths and high points.
- Invite students to read a certain number of their peers' final drafts and write paper or electronic Post-it comments.
- Share finished pieces on Google Docs for celebration and comments.
- Appoint several students to assemble an e-anthology.

Making Teacher Comments Count
#Didugetmymessage?

Laury Fischer, whose work you will read about in the next chapter, asks his students to write back to him after they have read the comments he writes on their papers. Fischer gives these instructions for the student letters that are addressed to him:

- Summarize the comments I made on your piece.
- What do you think about my comments?
- What are you going to do about them?

On subsequent papers, Fischer phrases his invitation this way:

- What did I say about your writing on the last paper?
- What did you do about it?

Fischer, an early participant and codirector of the Bay Area Writing Project, embraces this back-and-forth conversation with his students and the sheer practicality of having students keep track of their own progress. Asking students to reflect on the teacher's response to their work has added benefits. Meltzer (2010) points out that teaching students to set goals helps them "become independent learners" (p. 59). Research also indicates that students are better at managing the multiple demands of writing tasks when they learn how to set goals and plan (De La Paz, 2007; Graham, MacArthur, & Fitzgerald, 2013).

Using Reflections to Boost Discipline Vocabulary
#linkedin

Learning a discipline is often about learning key terminology. Judy Kennedy has discovered that she can link the terms she taught her students to their personal reflections—a marked departure from multiple-choice tests or other objective, abstract ways to test vocabulary.

As students are writing their final reflections for the How to Make a Living Project, Kennedy gives them a choice of 12 financial terms, ones that she has discussed in class. She asks students to choose three terms to include in their reflections and to explain what the terms mean and why they are important to that individual's financial future. Try it out for yourself: Where do these terms/concepts fit into your personal playbook: *taxable income*, *mutual funds*, *credit limit*, *identity theft*, *compound interest*, *APR*, *yearly deductible*, *bodily injury liability*, *investing*, *rate of return*, *credit score*, *IRA*?

CHAPTER 7

Writing to Think Critically

More than one teacher has had second thoughts about the conventional literary research project, even though its place in the high school curriculum often remains unchallenged. Is there a big payoff for all the hours both students and teachers devote to this endeavor?

Laury Fischer's moment of truth came when he was in a Bay Area Writing Project summer institute:

> I realized what I thought about research projects on authors like Ernest Hemingway. They were just everything they shouldn't be—impersonal and distant, written by unengaged students. But I was required to do papers like these with my seniors. What would happen, I wondered, if I just let them do their own thing? (Unless otherwise noted, all Fischer quotes are from a personal communication, August 15, 2018.)

Back in the world of school, Fischer decided to go with his hunch and allow students to select their own topics. However, that seemingly easy beginning brought up all kinds of dilemmas. Should the topics be related to literature? Should students pick an author? Should he provide an array of possible topics? Fischer got busy assembling a list. But one student (all it takes is one) resisted. "Do I have to do one of these?" he asked about the list. Fischer protested: "Isn't there a topic here for you?" "No, they all suck." Although he was on the spot, Fischer thought to ask, "What do you want to learn about?"

One thing Fischer was certain of as he stepped into the unfamiliar reality of student choice and the challenges it poses for both teacher and students: "I didn't want to call this new thing a research paper. That was dooming it. Somewhere I came up with the idea of the paper being protean." *Protean*, by the way, means "flexible," "versatile," "ever changing," "adaptable," "variable"—you get the idea. From these beginnings, the Proteus Project was born.

ABOUT THIS CHAPTER: CAPITALIZING ON CURIOSITY

The Proteus Project puts together many kinds of *writing to make an impact*, including narrative, civic action writing, and reflection. As a first-person research project that has worked in both high school and community college classrooms, it has passed the test of time. It also brings up issues that teachers face when they work with students on long-term projects. How to help select and investigate a topic? How to think critically about the topic, instead of merely reporting on it? How to work in opportunities for digital productions?

The second project we feature, "I Wish I'd Been There," was born in an American history class, where teacher Stan Pesick had his own frustrations with the required research paper. Like the Proteus Project, this one invites students to fire up their curiosity, imagination, and critical thinking skills and to make a personal connection with their topic.

At the heart of both projects is the idea of designing research projects that feed, rather than starve, students' curiosity. According to Ian Leslie (2014), curiosity begins early in life:

> Put a baby down anywhere, and it will start stroking, licking, picking things up and putting them in its mouth. . . . [T]he more actively a baby explores his or her environment, the more likely it is that he or she will go on to achieve academic success as an adolescent. (p. 23)

Adults become increasingly important when it comes to encouraging curiosity and the desire to learn: "As children grow older, their questions become more probing; they start to ask for explanations, rather than merely information" (Leslie, 2014, p. 27). Stimulating our students' interest may be one of our biggest contributions as teachers:

> Psychologist Paul Silvia explains that when people are interested in what they're reading, they pay close attention, process the information more efficiently, make more connections between new and existing knowledge, and attend to deeper questions raised by the text. . . . (Leslie, 2014, p. 82)

And now researchers can quantify the importance of curiosity to doing well in school. In addition to the traditional determinants of success—general intelligence and conscientiousness—*curiosity*—what Sophie Von Stumm (2011) calls "a hungry mind"—is the "third pillar of academic performance":

> [Von Stumm] hypothesized that *intellectual curiosity*—the tendency to "seek out, engage in, enjoy and pursue opportunities for effortful cognitive activity"—would count toward success, because students who possessed it would be hungry to learn information and explore new ideas. The data proved her right. . . . When put together, the personality traits of conscientiousness and curiosity count for as much as intelligence. (Leslie, 2014, pp. 81–82)

Curiosity doesn't lose its value after school:

> Employers are looking for people who can do more than follow procedures competently or respond to requests, who have a strong, intrinsic desire to learn

solve problems, and ask penetrating questions.
(Leslie, 2014, xvi)

> Curiosity is unruly. It
> doesn't like rules.
> —Ian Leslie

We might mention that students are not
the only ones whose curiosity is key to success.
Teachers like Fischer and Pesick put their own curiosity and imaginations to
work to create new possibilities for research projects. In addition to sharing
their projects, we describe their journeys.

CLASSROOM CLOSEUP: THE PROTEUS PROJECT
#multifaceted

A simple definition of the Proteus Project, according to Fischer, is a first-person
research project during which students read, conduct interviews, work inter-
actively, and, very importantly, come up with a critical question about their
chosen topic. Here's a quick summary of the components:

- Conduct firsthand research, including interviewing and observing.
- Read and cite at least eight print and digital sources.
- Engage in a participatory experience (optional).
- Carry out some kind of interactive work and use social media to
  complete the research.
- Ask a critical question about the topic, one that does not have a "yes"
  or "no" answer or maybe *any* answer.

In addition, Fischer asks his students to feel some passion about the topic
they select. His maxim: "Having fun is required. Remember: You're in love."
For examples of each of these requirements, see Figure 7.1.

Like most lists of requirements, this one developed over time and became increasingly sophisticated. Ultimately, Fischer came up with what he
believes makes this project different from other research papers or projects:
"I didn't want students to settle on a topic and simply write a report about
it. I wanted them to have a question about it so they would think and write
critically."

Before we examine each component more closely, let's look at one student
example to get an overview of what a Proteus Project could look like.

How One Student Tackled Proteus
#therealtest

Nineteen-year-old Jaden Washington easily met the condition that he fall in
love with his topic. As the son and nephew of airline pilots, he was considering
a career as a pilot. He decided to explore the idea that pilots might become
obsolete.

Figure 7.1. Proteus Project Components

READING (online and in print):

- Printed materials, databases, blogs, periodicals, journals
- Scholarly database articles (highly recommended)
- Required reading from at least one actual book
- Total reading (minimum): 8 resources (200 pages)

FIELDWORK A:

- Interviews with experts or other people. Two required.

FIELDWORK B (select three):

- *Observations:* Watching things—events, live performances, street theaters, fairs, community events, political events, lectures.
- *Participatory experience*: A participatory experience means *doing* something, not watching it done: Produce a CD; deprive yourself of technology for 3 days; march in a protest; eat only organic food for a week; apply to a modeling agency.
- *Interactive work*: Conduct an experiment, lead a class discussion, conduct a poll in class or online. Use social media.
- *Media produced by others*: Music, film, visual arts, audio arts, podcasts.
- *Media produced by you*: Creative expression—film, music, podcast, graphics, website, photographs. This can be part of the project and can be presented to the class.

Jaden begins his paper with a scenario that sets the scene for his critical question. Here is an excerpt:

"This is Your Auto-Captain Speaking at 30,000 Feet"
By Jaden Washington

"Good morning! Welcome aboard United Airlines flight 320" comes through the speakers of a United Airlines flight. David buckles his seatbelt and continues listening to the announcement. "This is your flight stewardess, Rachel, and today we will be flying from San Francisco to New York. The total flight time will be approximately 5 hours and 10 minutes. Our auto-captain will be pushing back from the gate soon, please make sure your tray tables are up and seatbelts are fastened as we prepare for takeoff." David leans back in his chair, slightly nervous as the plane pushes back from the gate and begins rolling on the taxiway toward the runway. This is his first time on a pilotless airline, and it has taken him quite a while to accept the idea of a flight with no human in the cockpit.

You probably noticed that this opening raises and dramatizes an issue and invites readers to think about how they might feel if they were locked in a tube without a human pilot. What comes next is Jaden's critical question, arising almost seamlessly from the story. The writer manages to avoid what young writers often do, that is, plunge an unsuspecting audience into a topic abyss without giving them any context or orientation:

Full automation in commercial airlines is seemingly on the horizon, and airlines supposedly could save billions by removing humans from the cockpits. What the industry must consider, however, is the comfortability of the public. A big question that must be asked is how can the public be made comfortable enough to buy tickets on these pilotless airlines?

Next comes an array of background information and expert opinion on public readiness for pilotless planes, including evidence of a critical pilot shortage. In total, Jaden quotes from nine sources.

What stands out for us is the amount of firsthand research that goes into a Proteus Project. In Jaden's case, he wanted to capture opposing ideas about whether or not the public could embrace the idea of planes without pilots. He interviewed an airline captain "to see what his opinion was on these autonomous planes in the future, and how he thinks the public would react." According to Jaden, the captain was not convinced that the pilotless plane will become a reality. Here's what the pilot had to say:

I don't see the public accepting it in the foreseeable future. How would a computer react in a catastrophic engine failure? . . . Every pilot union would be against it, both for the jobs of pilots and the safety of passengers. They would have to really prove that the computers are safer than humans. . . .

Pursuing another point of view, Jaden interviewed an aerospace engineer who believed wholeheartedly in the software and in a process for giving the flying public confidence. According to the engineer, "This technology wouldn't go out to the public until a company like Boeing is absolutely sure it would be safe . . . a big company with a big reputation must back it up."

One of the benefits of firsthand research is that the student writer takes a crack at being the authority. Notice in the excerpt below how conducting research using social media puts Jaden in charge. He collects and analyzes his own data, speaks with his own voice, and presents his own findings:

I conducted an online poll of four questions on the Instagram app to gauge the comfortability of the public with these ideas myself. After one day 800 people had responded to the poll, and the votes were in. The first question was "Would you be comfortable travelling in a driverless car". 298 people voted "yes" and 502 people voted "no", meaning that 62% percent voted for no, and 38% voted yes. The next question was "Would you be comfortable travelling in a pilotless commercial airplane?" and surprisingly, only 130 people voted "yes", and 670 people, or 83% voted "no". When the same question was asked again, but with a cheaper price of the plane ticket, 300 people voted for "yes" and 500 voted for "no".

In terms of *writing to make an impact*, Jaden is writing about something he has a personal interest in. He discovers the complexity of the topic as he goes along, reading about the fact that planes are already automated and potentially ready to go, while at the same time, the public is hesitant to give up a human in the cockpit. He has to dive into the pros and cons, but more, he has to explore what it would take to tip the balance for airline passengers. Cheap airfare? Maybe.

Finding a Topic
#fallinginlove

After years of supporting student choice, Fischer points out that it's not always so easy for students to manage a wide-open invitation without scaffolding. Often he paves the way by asking:

> What do you want to know more about, perhaps in the news or the sports world, in your personal life, or in religion? What are you curious about? What topic do you want to fall in love with? My favorite 2 days are when students write their lists. They give me topics to put on the board and by the end we have 90 ideas.

What surprises Fischer is the scope and substance of the topics:

> The range of what they write about is from the very personal to the offbeat to the political. It's open season—they see topics, share topics, steal topics, get inspired.

Student Matthew Yee chose a personal topic for his Proteus Project. In his introduction, he explains why this topic is important to him:

In my past, I have never even thought about what GMOs, Genetically Modified Organisms, are and didn't care whether or not I ate them, however that all changed on March of 2016 when my mother was diagnosed with cancer. When we got the news it was devastating and we were distraught for awhile, then we later became determined to do whatever we can to stop and prevent anymore damage from happening. In order to help, I started doing a lot of research and upon my research I stumbled on these organisms called GMOs and I continued to do a quick research on them. In my research I saw that there some health concerns that they can cause after eating such as toxins and while is not proven, there was said that it possible could cause cancer. After reading all of these factors my mom and I decided to make a new lifestyle choice and not eat or use any products that contain GMOs in order to remain any healthy as we can be.

Once students have a topic, they share it with members of their team, five or six other students with whom they meet for support. No one has to fly solo. According to Fischer, they know one another's topics, so they can look out for one another: "Usually, there's someone in the group who knows more about a topic than the person who has chosen the topic. They offer advice on where to get information, maybe a movie or blog or something online."

As for what counts as expertise, Fischer defines an expert as "anyone who knows so much more about the topic than you do. That could be a university professor or your uncle Bill or someone in class."

Asking a Critical Question
#exploration #openended #noeasyanswers

If finding a topic is difficult for students, asking a critical question (CQ) is even more difficult. Fischer introduces the idea in this way:

> In every other paper you've written, you've had a thesis statement. In this paper, you will have a thesis question and your paper will be an exploration. You don't have to end your paper by saying, "I know the answer." Your conclusion might be, "Here's what I'm thinking about this topic now."

One obvious hurdle for students is turning a topic into a critical question. Fischer provides models of how one becomes the other, a two-column chart with topics on the left and the corresponding critical question on the right (see Figure 7.2).

Since the entire project hinges on the critical question and assuming most students have not asked one before, Fischer has created eight litmus tests to head students in the right direction, or more likely, to keep them from stepping into potholes. For example, it's easy for students to end up with a "yes" or "no" question. As part of the litmus test, Fischer suggests that students try starting their questions with "To what extent." Another litmus test asks students if they already know the answer to their question, which would make it unsuitable. A particularly challenging litmus test is whether the critical question leads students to analyze, synthesize, and evaluate—the highest levels of thinking skills on Bloom's well-known taxonomy. (For a complete list of litmus tests, see Figure 7.3.)

Figure 7.2. Sample Proteus Topics and Critical Questions

Topic	Critical Question
Smiling	What accounts for the differences between the smiles of other cultures compared to the exaggerated American style?
Great art	What songs, art, movies, dances are universally loved? How come?
Service animals	How far should we allow people to go in bringing their animals into public places?
Forgiveness	To what extent can unforgiveable acts be forgiven? Should they be forgiven?
Sports	How should we define what constitutes a sport? What criteria define it?
Veterans' issues	If the American people are so thankful and proud of their troops, why isn't more done to address veterans' issues?
Training teachers	What are the best ways to train and predict who is going to be a good teacher? How much of teaching is personality?
Apathy	What accounts for my generation's apathy and ignorance about politics and the environment?
Being biracial	To what extent does being multiracial affect one's identity, mental health, and social and economic status?
View of the homeless	What accounts for the various reactions people have to the homeless?

Fischer's student Lukasz ("Hugo") Holdowicz, an immigrant to the United States, passes all of the litmus tests, including the need for open-endedness with his critical question: *When it comes to the issues with the immigration, why can't we find a middle ground on that topic?*

Similarly, student Cheyanne Moore's question—*Why and how is hip-hop and rap culture dominating the billboard charts and what are its effects on the current generation and how will it affect the future?*—passes all the litmus tests.

In some instances, however, the litmus tests are not enough. Recall Jaden and his inquiry into the public's willingness to fly without a pilot. Initially unable to nail down a critical question, he turned to Fischer for help:

Jaden came to my office one day, passionate about the topic, but without a good critical question. The question couldn't be "How do you become a pilot?" or "What's the hardest thing about being a pilot?" Too easy, no critical thinking. We got to talking and I asked him something like "What's the future of piloting?" And that's how he came to his question. (Personal communication, February 14, 2019)

Figure 7.3. Eight Proteus Litmus Tests

Yes-No Test	Is the CQ a yes/no question? **It shouldn't be.** Can you rephrase so that it is not a yes/no question? **"To what extent" sometimes works here.**
Been-There-Done-That Test	Does your CQ feel like it's been asked, discussed, and answered many times before? **It shouldn't.** Does the question feel fresh, new, and exciting? **It should.**
Open-Ended Speculation Test	Is your CQ open-ended, speculative, subject to fair dispute? **It should be.**
Hey, That's My Old Research Paper Test	Will the answer to your CQ create a conventional, familiar research paper (that is, based mostly on information available by reading)? **It shouldn't be.**
Critical Thinking Test	Will answering your CQ force you to do high-level, Bloom-worthy critical thinking (analysis, synthesis, evaluation)? **It should.**
Proteus Test	Are your topic and CQ well suited to the demands of the assignment? (a) traditional and Internet reading (b) interviewing (c) observing (d) Web 2.0ing (e) participating (f) critical thinking **It should be.**
Know-It-All Test	Do you (or almost everyone else) already know the answer to your CQ before you start your project? **The answer should be no.**
Passion Test	Where does your project fall on the passion-o-meter? Does your topic/CQ captivate, fascinate, and excite you? **It should.** Do you want to explore the answers to the CQ? **The answer should definitely be yes.**

Proteus Project Proposal
#planahead

Approximately a week after students have chosen a topic and tried their hand at a critical question, they submit a proposal outlining how they will address each part of the assignment. These are not absolute commitments, but preparing in this way with a written plan allows students to refine and ask questions and get rolling.

Nataly Berg begins her proposal by explaining how she came to her topic, crisis in the veteran community:

I became interested in this topic because I grew up surrounded by a military culture. I never really paid attention or was interested in learning who they are, what are their stories, and what are challenges they face. This changed when I encountered Sebastian Junger's TED Talk. "Our lonely society makes it hard to come home." Junger educated the audience about the reality that many Veterans are missing war life because they found in it a sense of brotherhood, a deep connection, protection, and safety. Values they do not find in our society today. These values are barely appreciated in our current society and instead individualism and division are rooted in the foundations of our systems.

To explore her critical question—*Despite the significant funding directed to veterans' medical programs, why is mental health in the veteran community in its current crisis?*—Nataly proposed the following:

- Three interviews with veterans who served in Kuwait, Iraq, and Israel
- Three kinds of readings, including a book, six articles, and a web version of the Department of Veteran Affairs budget for 2017, 2018, and 2019
- Four videos: TED Talk: "Our Lonely Society Makes It Hard to Come Home from War"; YouTube: "How to End Veteran Suicide"; documentary: *They Shall Not Grow Old*; movie trailer: *Korengal*
- Podcast: "Soldiers Say It's Hard to Return to Civilian Life"
- Observation: May 20 broadcast of *Veterans' Voices* focusing on shame and pride (accessed on Facebook Live)
- Participation: 9th Annual Healing Hearts 5K Walk/Run for Suicide Prevention

Several of the items in the proposal included additional explanation. For example, Nataly makes these notes about her participation in Healing Hearts:

I decided to sign up for "Healing Hearts" with a group of veterans to walk along their side to get to know them. I thought that in order to write about

Veterans I needed to genuinely listen to their feelings and concerns on mental health in their community. My intention as a civilian was to try to understand—in this limited time—their minds, hearts, and hopefully their needs more deeply.

We've included this abbreviated version of Nataly's proposal to give a general outline of a Proteus Project and a look at its trajectory. As for a critical question that has no single answer, the goal is that Nataly will swoop below the shallow surface of a tidy problem/solution. She ends her proposal this way:

My findings take me to reflect on the type of society we have become that Veterans are more scared to return home than staying at war. In what ways are we failing them? What can we do to help these warriors feel like their sacrifices mattered? What do people really mean when they say, "thank you for your service," when they have no idea what these sacrifices were?

Participating in an Experience
#divingin #offthesidelines

You may have noticed in Figure 7.1 that Fischer defines a participatory experience as "doing something, not watching it done." As an example, he recalls a young woman from Syria who was interested in how females are represented in the world. She narrowed her focus to the way Disney portrays women though fashion. Her experiment was to spend the day at a local shopping mall, dressed as a Disney princess. She brought along a friend to record people's reactions to her, some of which were positive and some decidedly less so.

Not all topics lend themselves to participation. For example, Jaden Washington, who explored what it would take to get the public to fly on pilotless airplanes, obviously did not have the possibility of flying on one himself. Participation isn't a fixed requirement. It's one of the options students can choose in Fischer's list of possibilities, many of which unchain students from their computers, getting them off the sidelines for direct, personal involvement. In investigating the question *What are the ethics and morals surrounding direct-to-consumer genetic testing/analysis companies selling and sharing their consumer data?* Georgia Moran found her participatory experience empowering: "I actually did my own genetic analysis test through 23andMe, in order to gain access to their systems and see what the setup was like."

> Active learning offers "meaningfulness, connection, interest, and purpose."
> —Jonas Soltis

How might participation be empowering? As an antidote to papers that merely regurgitate information, active participation is one way to move

students from a "surface approach" to learning into one aimed at the understanding of material: "a deep approach" ("Deep Learning, Surface Learning,"
1993, p. 10). Hands-on experience—learning by seeing how things work in
practice—also boosts the chances that the student will come away with more
confidence and authority—that old Mojo—to write as some kind of expert.
When students are empowered by a personal experience, they have a leg up
in shaping a reader's understanding of an issue or idea and of making an
impact.

The Benefits of Firsthand Research
#engagement #motivation #notjustgoogling

To what extent is it worth the time for students to engage actively as researchers, time that is spread out over weeks in Fischer's case? In a 2003 impact study
Bauer and Bennett found that students who had direct research experience in
their undergraduate education reported more "enhancement of their initiative
and communication skills" and development of their "intellectual curiosity"
than students who had no research experience. In particular, the long-term
benefits included the ability to obtain information independently, understand
research findings, and analyze literature critically (pp. 221–222). While this
survey focuses on the experiences of college students, acting as firsthand researchers will benefit high school students just as well.

Indeed, Fischer's students are the initiators, designers, conductors, and,
ultimately, interpreters of their own explorations. Case in point: Cheyanne
Moore interviewed three people whose opinions she valued when it comes
to hip-hop and its current and future influence. The first interviewee was her
mother, Talonna, whom Cheyanne identified as a baby boomer and "the one
who told me to choose this topic." Cheyanne asked Talonna, "How do you
think it's [hip-hop] going to affect the kids in the future?" Mom did not hold
back, stating her opinion that hip-hop has deteriorated from earlier days into
mumble rap—a sometimes derogatory term referring to incoherent lyrics:

To see what hip-hop has done to society already is shocking, I was able to
witness all stages of it because it initially started in the 80's. I think it's only
going to get worse over time, the lyrics are not even words, just a bunch of
mumble.

Now, like any bona fide researcher, Cheyanne, a huge fan of hip-hop, had
to figure out what to do with her interviewee's assertion that hip-hop has
deteriorated in lyrical prowess and substance. As a follow-up, she turned to
Instagram to conduct a poll among her followers. "Which rap music was more
meaningful to you, 1990s or now?" she asked. The results in some ways con-
firmed her mother's opinion. Cheyanne reported:

91% of my Instagram followers believe that rap music had more substance back in the 90's rather than today's rap. . . . Next, I asked my friends, my boyfriend, and coworkers the same question. The majority of feedback said that 90's rap music had more substance and it was more lyrical.

Cheyanne tested out her mother's claim one more time to confirm that the music in its current form might be "a bunch of mumble":

I observed my sister for 1 week and it was extremely difficult. For every song that she listened to I asked her to summarize what they were talking about. In this short week span, she approximately listened to about 40–50 rap songs. She was only able to summarize 1/3 of the lyrics.

In the end, Cheyanne completed seven readings, three interviews, one observation, and one Instagram poll, leading to her conclusion that while hip-hop is currently the largest genre in the country, it affects and influences people in both positive and negative ways, captivating individuals like her sister, while repelling others, represented by her mother.

When it comes to *writing to make an impact*, Cheyanne's experience speaks to the idea that the impact might also be on the student. Cheyanne—who said she aspires to some kind of career in hip-hop—cares about her topic, so her interviews and writeups have personal meaning, as does her discovery that her future career choice comes with some downsides. Her research is generative. What she finds out in one investigation—the interview with her mother—motivates her to conduct and report on another—the Instagram poll followed by the observation of her sister. Fischer describes Cheyanne's experience in glowing terms:

She was completely engaged by Proteus—the topic, the research, the writing. She became more and more motivated as the semester progressed. She had a great time writing her Proteus Project and ended up being a full Proteus superstar. (Personal communication, February 28, 2019)

Passion-o-meter
#5high1low

When students have finished their Proteus Projects, Fischer asks them to take a passion test to indicate the extent to which the topic they chose captivated, fascinated, and excited them: "How much do you adore-love-like-tolerate-despise your topic at this point?" He also asks about the level of their curiosity: "Did you actually want to explore the answers to the CQ [critical question]?"

Jaden gave his topic (pilotless airlines) a five, the top of the scale. Cheyanne affirmed that she would pick the same topic (hip-hop). Georgia, another young woman in Fischer's class who inquired about the ethics of genetic testing, gave her topic a five, but said she would not choose it again: "This was a rough topic—very broad. It was hard to narrow down what I wanted to write."

A passion-o-meter may sound—well—a little hokey. However, in terms of *writing to make an impact*, passion matters. So why not ask about it? What matters is the extent to which students care about the writing and are committed to doing what it takes to get to the finish line.

A Final Note: Negotiating
#bargaining #tradeoffs

You may recall that Fischer, then a high school teacher, began his journey with Proteus by wondering what would happen if he let students "do their own thing." The idea was risky, not just because of potential bedlam in his own classroom, but also because "I knew I'd get a pushback from my colleagues." The prevailing opinion, as it might be today, was that kids should "stay in the lane" and do the orthodox, longstanding, time-honored, hidebound research paper.

Obviously, Fischer took the risk and then later went even further, inviting students to negotiate the requirements of the Proteus Project. Open to swapping one thing for another, he was willing to customize wherever possible. Here is how he describes his approach:

> Make me an offer. Want to do seven interviews and half the reading? Let's talk. Want triple the maximum length of the paper (as one student did)? Make me a spectacular offer. Want to make a short movie and not do any interviews? Let's make a deal. . . . One Proteus slogan: "Everything in the Proteus Project is negotiable. But everything must be negotiated." Meaning I'll listen to any offer they want, but I won't always say "yes." A student last semester asked if he could make a movie documenting his project and not hand in a paper. Answer? No. (Personal communication, February 13, 2019)

This kind of open-ended negotiation may be too burdensome in the world where teachers and students have six or seven class periods, or some other demanding daily combination. Certainly, we are not advocating a lot of deal-cutting. But it's worth noting that some negotiation—or a buffet of choices—puts the writing task more squarely in the writer's corner, with perhaps more possibility that the writing will have an impact on the one in charge—the student. It's a balancing act, but for sure, students tend to be more motivated when they have some degree of choice and decisionmaking. How important is motivation? In *How Learning Works*, the authors tell us that "students' motivation generates, directs, and sustains what they do to learn" (Ambrose, Bridges, Lovett, DiPietro, & Norman, 2010, p. 69).

When Laury Fischer unpledged his allegiance to "The Research Paper," he had to invent something else. Something that would play into a student's natural and individual sense of curiosity. Something that would result in writing unlike the writing that typically accompanies traditional assignments: "impersonal and distant, written by unengaged students" was the way Fischer described it. In the end, he replaced what was distant from students' lives with a project that piqued their curiosity and imagination and led them to explore without having to nail down the traditionally required definitive answer. In the process, students actually expanded their repertoire of research techniques and wrote with authority and conviction.

According to Kathleen Blake Yancey and her colleagues Liane Robertson and Kara Taczak (2014), we might want to rethink assignments like the research paper in preparation for college academic writing:

> In this moment in composition, teachers and scholars are especially questioning two earlier assumptions about writing: (1) that there is a generalized genre called academic writing and (2) that we are teaching as effectively as we might. (p. 2)

The alternative, they write, is to give students the "writing knowledge and practices that they can draw upon, use and repurpose for new writing tasks in new settings" (p. 2). In other words, the idea of the one-way road to academic writing has dead-ended.

In the next classroom closeup, notice that high school history teacher Stan Pesick comes up with a new vision for having his students write up their research, one that exists in the world where real historians write for real audiences and hope to engage them, rather than putting them to sleep.

CLASSROOM CLOSEUP: "I WISH I'D BEEN THERE"
#flyonthewall

When he began to teach 11th-grade history in Oakland, Pesick (2001b) struggled with what his students wrote as they tried their hand at the required research paper: "Needless to say, the papers I received were generally boring.... The student's voice was absent. The papers lacked the detail, the sense of story, and the committed voice of the historian" (p. 1).

Like Fischer, he wanted to shake things up, but how to do so was the question of the hour. Before he stumbled into an assignment that changed the way he taught, he went on to invent something even worse. Pesick decided to have everyone write on the same topic. This approach would allow him to take his students through all the readings and processes simultaneously. The result was most unfortunate: "I received sixty versions of the paper that all said the same thing. Once again, individual engagement and voice were missing. Imagine correcting sixty copies of the same paper and hearing the sound of 60 voices never hitting the right key" (2001b, p. 3).

Creating a New Vision
#witnessinghistory

In many ways, history teachers face a fierce headwind whenever they try to reimagine what writing about history could look like in school. Good models, as they exist in school, are scarce. Pesick laments, "The textbooks students read are a set of declarative statements. They don't point students in the direction of asking 'What's the story?' 'Why did happen?' 'What's going on here?'"

The firmly ingrained school version of a research paper generally asks students to read about a topic and report on what they read: the given information. The research and writing combine to create a closed circle. The student simply records the given information and passes it back to the teacher.

No surprise, the goal of writing a research papers often gets reduced to learning how to quote from the text or learning how to set up citations. The real meat of history gets lost: Wondering about people's motives and feelings. Considering the role of social context. Wondering about the way people lived. Questioning why things happened the way they did. Wanting to know more.

In Pesick's case, a new model for writing about history showed up as he was reading an article in *American Heritage*. The magazine editors had asked a number of historians and writers this question: "What is the one scene or incident in American history you would like to have witnessed—and why?" Pesick found their responses "interesting, moving, thoughtful, and personal." He heard the historian's voice, so often missing in school writing about history. Here's an example of what Pesick read:

> The incident that I would have witnessed is that described in Thomas Wentworth Higginson's *Army Life in a Black Regiment*. He writes of a ceremony in South Carolina on January 1, 1863, celebrating the coming into effect of the Emancipation Proclamation. The ceremony was conventional and simple until Higginson got up to speak and waved the American flag before the audience of black soldiers, white civilians and officers, and a large number of slaves, who at the moment were legally receiving their freedom for the first time. As the flag was being waved, Higginson tells us, "there arose . . . a strong male voice (but rather cracked and elderly), into which two women's voices instantly blended, singing, as if by an impulse that could no more be repressed than the morning note of the song sparrow, 'My Country, 'tis of thee, Sweet Land of Liberty, of thee I sing!'"
>
> The ceremony ended as the former slaves sang on, irrepressibly, through verse and verse. Higginson motioned the few whites who began to join in to be silent.

The moment, as he said, was electric. "Nothing could be more wonderfully unconscious; art could not have dreamt of a tribute to the day of jubilee that should be so affecting; history will not believe it . . ." This incident epitomizes the most profound moment in America's social history: that point when millions ceased to be slaves in the home of the free and set in motion the historic challenge that white America make real its own vision. (Carl N. Degler, as cited in "I Wish I'd Been There," 1984)

Don't miss the first line of this piece. The writer uses the first-person pronoun: "I would have witnessed. . . ." Emancipation! Then the story: an unadorned ceremony interrupted by a soloist—perhaps past his prime—and ultimately, the voices of those who knew the words by heart and whose freedom would launch "the historic challenge." In two short paragraphs, the writer gives us context, facts, description, narration, and significance.

When Pesick read this piece and others like it, he was hooked. Of course, he would ask more of his students than two paragraphs, but the rationale and pattern, plus the gift of a human voice, were in place.

Engaging Students in Historical Research
#writinghistory

When Pesick imagined students selecting a moment in history to write about, he was on his way to a new framework for teaching historical significance. No longer would the teacher be the only authority. The students themselves would need to think about what events were compelling to them and why. They would also need "factual knowledge and criteria for sorting the significant from the insignificant" (Pesick, 1998, p. 232).

How Students Worked with Historical Significance

In passing the baton to his students, Pesick (2001a) asked them at the beginning of the year to make a list of what they considered to be significant events and individuals in American history—a list they would return to and revise based on what they learned during the semester:

I knew that students arrived in my class with many fragments of historical knowledge gathered from previous classes, family stories, and accounts of the past in popular culture. I speculated that one way for students to build a personal connection to the past would be to put this information and misinformation to use. Students could revise, refine, and supplement what they already knew. I reasoned that they would be able to do this if I allowed them more room to explore and write about their initial responses to historical events and individuals. I began to encourage—actually require—students to write about what they found interesting and significant from the textbook and other sources and to jot down questions about what troubled and confused them. (pp. 131–132)

To help students understand the idea of historical significance, Pesick (1998) gave them the following task:

Select a total of five important individuals, groups, or events that you would regard as historically significant. (p. 167)

To justify each of their selections, Pesick supplied two criteria: (1) significant events and people have a profound impact, whether positive or negative, on the lives of individuals and groups in a particular time period; and (2) significant events and people are relevant to our understanding of the past, but also to our understanding of the present.

When students have the go-ahead to experiment with the notion of historical significance, what kinds of situations attract or have an impact on them? Pesick (2001a) notes that his students gravitated toward events "about which they could make moral judgments and express empathy with those who have been wronged" (p. 144). Notice student Mandy's outrage in her comments about a newfound historical hero:

Ida B. Wells: I admired the courage and spirit of Ida B. Wells when she didn't get out of her chair which she was told to by a white man. My reactions were 'You go girl!' I had to say that because there's hardly any 4 ½ feet tall female could stand up for herself back in those days. Even today in America many foreigners give up their dreams and live under people's shoes. Wells was little but she became one of the famous leaders against lynching and stop the murdering of blacks by whites. The years gone by, she became a full time writer and expressed the bitter feelings inside of her about racism. She fought many ways to lead African Americans to a better condition of life. (Pesick, 2001a, p. 135)

In terms of historical significance, Mandy's writing links the past and the present. It also shows that she is learning to make judgments about what is important in history and to understand time periods and social contexts different from her own.

Recall that Pesick is ultimately looking for the kind of writing he found in the piece "Emancipation," which begins with a personal selection of one historical moment and includes evidence of why that moment is significant. To come closer to this kind of historical understanding, Pesick offers his students the opportunity to revise their early reactions to an historical event, and apply what they have learned over the semester. In the excerpt below, Patty recounts her initial response to the burning of a British tax collector's home during the period leading up to the revolution. She is indignant over the unfairness of this act:

> The Event I reacted to . . .
>
> Tensions ran high during the period of the colonists' rebellion. The colonists were angered at the British rule over them and the mob's burning and destruction is a result of that anger. In particular the burning of a British tax collector, Andrew Oliver's house. When I first read about this event I was appalled at how, even though they were angry, the colonists could destroy the life of a man who merely represented but did not cause the problems of the British rule. However, as I read more and began to understand what the colonists were experiencing and what Andrew Oliver truly represent I partially changed my mind on the event. This is why I chose this reaction, so that I could have the chance to go back and revise my original thinking. (Pesick, 1998, p. 234)

In this piece, Patty explains that in her first writing about this historical event she reacted strongly to the injustice of the mob action. Given the chance to learn more and to revise, she reconsiders the violent mob action as horrifying but "understandable":

> My revision . . . The burning and destruction of Andrew Oliver's house represents a horrible yet necessary time in history. Andrew Oliver, a representative of the British government, was in the colonies to collect taxes which Britain had imposed on the colonies. When these colonists began to realize how much control their government had over them their only reaction was anger. Andre Oliver and others like him became a symbol of everything the colonists saw as wrong with their government. As Britain taxed more and more, the colonists became more angry and so many outright rebellions occurred. From this came the destruction of Andre Oliver's house. Although it was awful that Oliver's house was destroyed it is understandable why the colonists were so angry and why they needed someone to use to make their point. The point they made was heard loud and clear by Britain because of rebellions such as this one. So just like the time period in they occurred these rebellions were horrible but necessary to the success of the country. (Pesick, 1998, p. 234)

> You will not have written a history paper if you report something happened. Rather, a history paper explores how and why something happened and its significance.
> —Mary Lynn Rampolla

Writing to learn, as Mandy and Patty have done, is "a tool for discovering, for shaping meaning, and for reaching understanding" (Fulwiler & Young, 1982, p. x). What matters here is the blueprint:

- Students base their writing on their own interests. They select incidents in history that jump out at them as important or meaningful in some way. They write to discover and understand, but they also write to capture a bit of history as their own. In a discipline that often seems unwelcoming to students, writing gives them "a place for curiosity and imagination, a place to get in their own two cents." (Pesick, 2019)
- Students revise when they've learned more about people and events in history. In their revisions, they move toward a more nuanced understanding of how their chosen incident affects other people's lives, its impact in the past and the present.
- By becoming more personally involved in historical moments, students develop the strong, personal voice that Pesick found so compelling in the "Emancipation" model. They begin to use historical thinking skills like narration, analysis, and interpretation.
- With the experience of learning about historical significance, students have the way into "I Wish I'd Been There."

WRITING HISTORY
#connectingwiththepast

With the experience of writing and learning about historical significance, Pesick's students had the map they would need for his new research assignment, "I Wish I'd Been There." As you look over this assignment in Figure 7.4, notice its goals are in line with all the preparation work:

> This assignment became the course's culminating writing assignment. The assignment in which I really wanted students to "write history." The assignment in which they constructed an historical account by choosing and describing an event and working with historical evidence. In addition, the students would also, as they constructed the account, analyze its significance and interpret its meaning. This kind of historical writing is my ultimate goal for students, but I also have a more humble goal. I don't want my students to tell a history teacher they might meet many years from now that they hated history. This is a comment I have heard from too many individuals too many times. Ultimately these two goals are really inseparable and are connected to the day-to-day instruction in my classroom. (Pesick, 2001b, p. 7)

You might notice that Pesick's approach to moving away from the dry research paper is to invite students to bring the past to life in the present. He appeals to students to make a personal connection, create a romance with their topic. Above all, he wants the assignment to lead to writing that students will value.

Figure 7.4. The Fly on the Wall Assignment

"I WISH I'D BEEN THERE"

What is the one scene or event in American history you would like to have witnessed—and why?

- Start your work on this assignment by selecting a photograph, illustration, painting, video, or graphic/cartoon of a significant event that you would like to have witnessed.
- Develop an historical inquiry question about the event that your paper (3–5 pages) will seek to answer.

To answer your historical question, you should:

1. Describe what you see in the photograph, illustration, painting, video or graphic/cartoon.
2. Discuss the event's historical context—what led up this moment and what came after? (For this part, read and/or view historical accounts of the time period surrounding the event.)
3. Explain how various people at that time responded to the historical moment in the photograph, video, or illustration. (For this part, use primary source documents or evidence cited in historical pieces about the event, to find out what people at that time thought.)
4. Explain why the moment you selected is significant in American history.
5. Discuss why this moment so intrigued you.

In some way, his students have to put themselves in the scene, explaining that from where they stand, this is what they see. For example, one of his students chose to be among the marchers during the March on Washington on August 28, 1963. Another put himself in the stands when Babe Ruth called his shot, pointing to center field, where he hit a home run, in the fifth inning of game three of the 1932 World Series at Chicago's Wrigley Field. For yet another student, the scene at Iwo Jima compelled her to ask herself what the men were feeling at the time they raised the flag. (To her great dismay, she found out that the picture was posed.) Whether sitting on the bus next to Rosa Parks in 1955, or standing on the lawn as Japanese family members leave their home in 1942, students position themselves in a time and place that grabs their attention.

Curiosity and Critical Questions

In Pesick's view, a series of factual statements about the past, however precise they may be, does not add up to a history paper. "You will not have written a history paper if you simply report that something happened," he tells his students (Pesick, 2019). Like Fischer, Pesick wants his students to ask a critical question, what he calls an "historical inquiry question," that will, in effect, turn his students into explorers. One object of their search is to uncover different points of view and to look for evidence about who was affected by the event and to what extent.

> Gradually students learn that any historical grain, even one in their own history, reflects the larger context in which it took place and can be made to speak to important questions in the past and the present.
> —Marjoleine Kars

Like Fischer, Pesick is in the market for questions with no easy-to-research, definitive answers, questions that emerge from a strong desire to know or learn something. Here are two examples:

> How did Japanese Americans endure the hardships of what happened to them during World War II?
> Why do Americans seem so obsessed by the Vietnam war? (Pesick, 2019)

It's questions like these that Pesick hopes will encourage students to care about history and take a more nuanced view of it.

Notable Classroom Practices
#studentsatthecenter

In addition to their unique value as approaches to research, the Proteus Project and the "I Wish I'd Been There" Project share several classroom practices in common that cater to student choice, authority, engagement, and voice. Both Pesick and Fischer ask their students to write about what ignites their curiosity. Both teachers draw on students in the class to act as audience and to provide support.

We have linked their parallel practices in Figure 7.5 to make this point: Whether or not Fischer and Pesick were thinking specifically about *writing to make an impact*, they increased the odds that the tasks they came up with would produce writing and writing experiences that mattered.

Figure 7.5. Classroom Practices That Support Writing to Make an Impact

Practices	Proteus Project	I Wish I'd Been There
Have students choose a topic that matters to them.	Students choose a topic that plays to their curiosity, passion, or concerns.	Students select an event that piques their curiosity and has historical and personal significance.
Help students engage with their chosen topic.	Students share their topics and resources in whole-class and small-group settings, enhancing the meaningfulness and effectiveness of the topic.	Students share their topics in whole-class and small-group settings, intensifying their curiosity about how profoundly the event affected people's lives.
Make the writing a personal journey.	Students are in charge of interviewing, using social media, and participating in an experience.	Students develop historical empathy by finding out about moments, ideas, and events in the past and how these connect to us collectively and individually today.
Invite students to have a personal point of view.	Students write in the first person, interpret their own research, and weigh different perspectives.	Students offer their personal interpretations of the significance of their chosen historical events.

TEACHING PLAYBOOK

Both Fischer and Pesick emphasize the irreplaceable role of student curiosity, especially when students are faced with doing a research project. No doubt about it, curiosity is a driving force, and as we all know, it starts at a very young age with incessant questions like "why, why, why?" While asking questions comes naturally when children want to know something, interviewing—even though it can be spontaneous—takes some front-end planning and practice.

Learning to Interview
#tellmemore

For students who are learning to interview, parents, grandparents, and other trusted adults are handy as interviewees. They tend to talk a lot because they are glad for the chance, and in most cases, they are a safe bet. Kids can learn the ropes of interviewing with someone they know before they have to branch out. We also believe that students—much as they might like to ignore what their parents have to tell them—are deeply interested in how the adults around them operate and what they think.

You may recall that Laury Fischer's student Cheyanne interviewed her mother as part of her Proteus Project about the current and future influences of hip-hop. In fact, Fischer recalls that Cheyanne chose her topic "mostly because she got to include mom. How cool is that?" (personal communication, February 28, 2019).

We preface our two learning-to-interview examples (one English and one social studies) with a few general guidelines. We have found these helpful in our own work and our teaching of students who may never have interviewed before. Here is one way to frame the guidelines for your class:

Getting Ready for Your Interview

1. Plan your questions ahead and line them up in single file. A layered question like the following is great as a critical question, but too long and complicated for an interview: "What is your experience with hip-hop and how do you think it will affect this generation and future generations to come?" Break this question into thirds for better results.
2. Deviate from your plan by listening carefully to your interviewee and asking follow-up questions. The initial list of questions is important as a guide, but some of the best information comes from impromptu questions like "What made you feel that way?" or "What happened next?"
3. Keep in mind that you want open-ended questions that get to the "why" or "how." Stay away from questions that can be answered "yes" or "no." Instead of "Was this important?" ask "Why was this important?" or "How do you explain . . ." or "I'd like to hear about. . . ."

One more bit of advice: It's worth taking time to practice interviewing in class in whatever way makes sense—with student partners or with a whole-class interview of someone. Be sure to reflect and comment on what questions worked best and why.

Interviewing Exercise #1: What did you do in high school, Dad?

When students interview one of their parents or another trusted adult about their high school years, they get two lessons for the price of one. The first, of course, is personal—a glimpse of the adolescent life of someone they care about. If things go right, the second is a shot at learning how to interview and learning how empowering it is to conduct your own research. We suggest pairing the interview assignment with a book that deals with teenage years, typically around high school.

Here are some book recommendations:

Eleanor & Park by Rainbow Rowell
Me, Earl, and the Dying Girl by Jesse Lewis
Harry Potter and the Goblet of Fire by J. K. Rowling
The Outsiders by S. E. Hinton
The Pigman by Paul Zindel
The Chocolate War by Robert Cormier
A Separate Peace by John Knowles
The Absolutely True Diary of a Part-Time Indian by Sherman Alexie
The Catcher in the Rye by J. D. Salinger

Rather than asking students to write some kind of literary analysis after they have read the book, invite them to examine the themes of adolescence through another lens—one that is closer to their own lives—by conducting an interview. As a change of pace, it's probably more interesting for students to expand on a theme than to rehash it. That said, the real goal of this assignment is for students to learn a skill they can use in any number of writing situations.

We offer these classroom-tested sample interview questions. You may want to add to these, or change them entirely. Themes/issues that crop up in books about adolescence like isolation, alienation, insecurity, popularity, learning to be yourself, picking the right friends—these are all fodder for teachers and students to generate their own interview questions.

- Where did you go to high school? When?
- How did you get to school?
- What did you wear back then?
- How was the attitude toward school? Why did kids like it? What did they not like about it?
- What were the required subjects?
- What were the expectations for boys? For girls?
- How did sports fit into high school life? What about girls' sports?
- What kind of activities came along with school?
- What did school spirit look like?
- How did students treat one another? Examples?
- In what ways did you feel pressure to get good grades? To fit in with your peers?
- How do you think school life has changed? In what ways for the better? In what ways for the worse?

Credit for this assignment idea goes to Ken Lane, a former high school teacher and preservice teaching supervisor at the University of California, Berkeley. It became popular in the early days of the Bay Area Writing Project after Lane shared it with his colleagues. For students, the interviewing exercise comes with a payoff. They have at their fingertips a lot of content for writing or presentations: human interest stories, glimpses of high school then and now, insights into changing values, or the ways things have remained the same. Armed with specific details (some of them laugh-worthy), students have good stuff for *writing to make an impact*.

Interviewing Exercise #2: Managing Credit Cards

Our second exercise comes from Judy Kennedy's Make a Living Project in her 12th-grade economics class (see Chapter 6, p. 83). As part of their hands-on financial literacy experiences, students must interview a parent or another adult who has had a credit card for at least 5 years, someone who has been around the block and lived through good and bad times with a credit card. Here are some sample questions, ones that Kennedy's students use and build on:

- What do you like about credit cards?
- What do you dislike about credit cards?
- How do you decide what credit card to get?
- How many credit cards have you had at one time, including cards from stores?
- Do you still use those cards? Why or why not?
- What kinds of purchases do you make with your credit cards?
- Why don't you use cash, checks, money orders, or other forms of payment for those purchases?
- How do you pay your credit card bill? Do you pay a minimum every month? A set amount? The whole thing? What's your strategy?
- What advice would you give a person who is getting a credit card for the first time?

Kennedy advises students to get detailed answers, which they will need for the next step in this exercise. The writeup includes the following:

Introduction: Write about the person you interviewed, explaining why you selected this particular interviewee. Include two or three interesting things about the person.
Question and Answer: Write out each question you asked and the response.
Reflection: Explain what stood out for you in this interview and why. What did you learn?

Students share what they learned first with partners and then with the entire class. Kennedy reports that for many students, this interview experience is one of the highlights of the Make a Living Project: "Kids and parents take it very seriously. They get to have a conversation about money. Kids find out things they never knew, even that some parents have filed for bankruptcy."

Here is another example of two lessons for the price of one. On one hand, students learn how to conduct an interview. On the other, students discover some realities about credit cards, but not from just anyone or from an article or textbook. Their experts are people they know well and the answers have personal significance.

Interviewing Exercise #3: Oral History

Imagine sitting down with a friend or family member and asking about past events—important moments that person has lived through—with a recorder or video camera capturing the interview. Conducting and writing up oral histories makes an impact in a big way when students connect what has gone before them to their lives at the moment:

> Explaining and understanding the past connects us to our families, communities and country. We probably can never really fully understand those who lived before us, but the effort helps us understand our society, and perhaps finally, ourselves. (Guidelines for Oral History Interviews, 2018, para. 2)

One oral history assignment that has worked especially well for us comes from Studs Terkel (1997), the great oral historian, and his classic book, *Working: People Talk About What They Do All Day and How They Feel About What They Do*. (A more modern graphic adaptation of *Working* is also available; see Pekar and Buhle, 2009.) While the original book is dated, the voices of real working people ring true, even if their titles have changed over the years—for example, *airline stewardess* is now *flight attendant*. Terkel offers a wide range of interviews with workers such as a mail carrier, waitress, baseball player, hooker, stockbroker, garbage man, and farm worker. For those who are unfamiliar with this classic book, be forewarned that there are fewer women represented than men and it's short on cultural and ethnic diversity. (Remember that oral history preserves different time periods and events.) Here's the big plus: The interviews are easy, fun, and instructive. They serve as models for writing up an oral history and as a pre-interviewing tool for coming up with questions.

Our suggestion is to select several relevant interviews from the book to look at and discuss together as a class. Here are some questions you might ask:

- What kinds of questions do you think Terkel asked to get this story?
- What are some examples? For instance, Terkel might have asked, "What was one of your most eventful days?" or "Tell me a funny thing that happened to you on the job."

- What makes the interview compelling? Consider these attributes: a real voice, direct quotes, authentic stories, a fresh understanding of the job and how it impacts the person who does it.
- Terkel crafted his interviews into personal narratives. Which ones stand out for you and why?

After these class discussions, if you have the book or ebook, you can let the students browse through interviews that interest them. If you have time, you might want to have one more talk about which interviews appealed most and why.

At this point, students are somewhat ready to identify a person to interview about his or her job. Once they have someone in mind, it's useful to develop the interview questions together, depending on how experienced the students are. When they have completed the interview with all their notes and/or transcripts, they can turn to the book for ample models for the writeup. The student's task is to select from all the things their interviewee tells them and to make a story from those selections, using the interviewee's words.

> Students seldom get the chance to act as historians who record and interpret history for themselves and for others. Historians often act like detectives who are trying to solve intriguing puzzles.
> —Guidelines for Oral History Interviews

Our best advice at this point: Don't just settle for what we have offered here. Check out the Internet for more ideas for oral history projects, including topics and guidelines. They are everywhere! Here are some examples:

www.tellmeyourstories.org/sample/
www.tolerance.org/classroom-resources/student-tasks/do-something/oral-history-project
www.edutopia.org/living-legends-oral-history-projects-bring-core-subjects-to-life

Using Artifacts to Develop Topics
#concreterepresentations

Several times in this book, we have argued against treating a lesson or playbook exercise as a one-shot, something to be pulled out of a hat on a rainy day, never to appear again. But here is an exercise that can make a single appearance. Aside from its value for learning, it has two other tremendous advantages: It takes only one class period at most and it doesn't require grading.

We watched this exercise in action in Laury Fischer's class, where students were modifying and solidifying their Proteus Project topics. They arrived in class, each carrying an artifact that was to represent in some way the topic they were developing. The room smelled of fresh-baked cookies (an edible artifact depicting low carbs recommended on the Keto diet). Among other artifacts: an outdated grammar book (standing for the way social media has impacted traditional grammar rules); a map of Mars showing the best places to colonize; an empty pill bottle exemplifying the life-changing realities of early-onset diabetes.

Then came the assignment:

- What exactly did you bring? Describe your artifact.
- Why this artifact? How is your artifact a symbol, metaphor, or representation of your Proteus topic?

The next steps combine writing, talking, listening, questioning, thinking, and rethinking:

- Free write about the artifact for 5 minutes.
- Discuss the artifact's significance in small groups.
- Ask one another questions about how the artifact reflects what the writer wants to accomplish with the topic.

What strikes us about the use of artifacts as a tool for drilling down on a topic or question is its very specific intellectual purpose. Bringing artifacts to class is nothing new. They serve a myriad of objectives, such as building community, encouraging cultural awareness, and reflecting on who we are as individuals or members of families. In contrast, Fischer's use of artifacts is intended to push students toward fruitful topics and critical questions.

Similarly, Stan Pesick uses artifacts to jump-start his American history students in their search for a topic. As you read earlier, his assignment begins with students selecting a photo, painting, or illustration of a significant event they would like to have witnessed. Starting with a representation of an event or scene not only helps students find a topic, but also shape it. Pesick (2019) explains: "There needed to be a way to help students narrow the topic into something very manageable in a short paper." With artifacts, students had "something very concrete to explore." Rather than being at D-Day, students could now be on the beach at Normandy; rather than being in Montgomery during the bus boycott, students could now be on the bus with Rosa Parks or in a church with Martin Luther King. The photo was a great aid in narrowing the topic.

Levstik and Barton (1997) promote the use of artifacts in the teaching of history:

> We cannot overstate the importance of using visual images (particularly photographs) . . . visual sources tap into a much wider range of background knowledge than printed text or oral discussions. (p. 86)

These authors also find a significant element of authenticity when teachers use some kind of photo or other artifact to help students understand and interpret historical events. After all, we often look at tangible objects to explore history in our everyday lives:

> Outside school, people really do take an interest in how things have changed over time: People save artifacts and photographs, and they tell their children and grandchildren how things were different in the past. (p. 87)

For today's students, images they find online might broaden the kind of artifacts they work with—for example, moments in history accessed on YouTube, TED Talks about ideas worth spreading, or Podcast audio stories and programs. These pack a different kind of punch and engagement because they combine both the visual and auditory to produce drama, action, comedy, music, and art—in other words, the stuff of life, present and past.

Demonstrating Critical Thinking
#marginnotes

Fischer has an easy, handy technique to find out what students know and how they actually use what they know. To cement their learning of analysis and synthesis, he asks his students to indicate in margin notes on their reports where they have used these thinking skills.

We like this idea for several reasons. First, by identifying critical thinking skills in their margin notes, students can make them conscious and retrievable. We also like margin notes for their flexibility as a learning and teaching tool. Teachers—ourselves included—have used them or can use them for all kinds of writing skills and strategies. Here are some examples and a way to present them to students:

Mark and comment on a place in your writing where you did the following:

- Used your own voice
- Made a claim
- Delivered a thesis statement
- Featured evidence to support a claim and interpreted the evidence for your reader
- Told an illustrative story
- Summarized
- Made your best transition
- Used "show not tell"
- Included a cool fact
- Incorporated a specific example
- Persuaded your reader

You can also have students trade papers and ask a partner to identify where certain features show up. This gives the student writer a chance to see whether and where a reader finds a given strategy. We have used this technique with thesis statements and found that many times, after swapping papers, the reader either can't locate the thesis statement or selects a sentence different from the one the writer intended. In our experience, the real value is in the discussion that follows, either between partners or with the entire class. Students seem more willing to go back to the drawing board when a peer has reviewed their work.

CHAPTER 8

Conclusion

If you could thumb through a folder of all the writing you did in high school or college, which piece would stand out as your proudest or most meaningful? What was it about the writing or the writing experience that separates this paper from all the others?

Professor James Lang, for one, had an occasion to visit his basement several decades after his undergraduate years at Notre Dame. He was moving with his family to a new home and rifling through boxes to decide what to keep and what to toss. When he came upon a yellow folder of papers from his college days, he was not particularly surprised to find many that he never even remembered writing, nor did he remember many of the classes themselves.

But one essay caught his eye. He knew he had saved it: a 20-page analysis of the film *My Dinner with Andre*. "I was immensely proud of that paper," he remembered, "since I had conceived the topic entirely on my own in response to a very open-ended essay prompt. It gave me an opportunity to explore creative issues that had been preoccupying me since high school...." (Lang, 2017, para. 5).

Eodice, Geller, and Lerner (2017) asked more than 700 undergraduates from three different institutions to describe a meaningful writing project from their undergraduate years and to explain why they selected it. From this survey, three attributes of a meaningful writing assignment rose to the surface, attributes we have explored at different points in this book as pathways to *writing to make an impact*:

1. *Give students a say.* Most meaningful assignments give students "opportunities or freedom to pursue topics of interest, to connect those topics to what they had passion for or had experienced, and to map their meaningful writing projects to their future writing and professional identities" (Eodice et al., p. 33).
2. *Engage students actively, not passively.* A passive writing assignment is one in which students write individually about content they have studied in class or found from research. In the end, the student turns in the paper.

   An active writing assignment, on the other hand, allows students to be interactive during the writing process (for example, with teacher and peer feedback); they conduct firsthand research such as interviews; they link their projects to personal experience and know exactly to whom they are writing.

3. *Give students writing experiences that transfer.* In this case, *transfer* means creating assignments that invite students to use things they have already learned in a new writing situation (for example, using narrative in a new genre like Pesick's "I Wish I'd Been There.") It also means offering assignments that help students develop skills that will transfer to future writing (such as learning poetic writing skills that positively affect multiple kinds of writing).

The authors of *The Meaningful Writing Project* emphasize that not every writing assignment will necessarily contain equal doses of all three attributes. Instead, they suggest that we look for "the places where aspects of a writing assignment can be made more expansive, more inviting, more past connected, and more future-oriented in ways driven by students' goals and interests" (Eodice, Geller, & Lerner, 2017, p. 136).

EXPANDING WRITING TASKS AND EXPERIENCES

Increasingly, writing is a public and even collaborative act, but school often keeps ideas walled off from the world, shared only between student and teacher, and sometimes only shared between student and an anonymous grader. It's almost worse than having students practicing the training wheels version of writing. It's more like we haven't even let them on a bike. (Warner, 2018, pp. 16-17)

As teachers who have offered our share of narrow, show-me-what-you-learned writing assignments, we know that "meaningful" is a slippery, subjective measure. That said, we take seriously the scenario that Kelly Gallagher (2011) paints when he admonishes us to find valuable purposes for the writing we ask our students to do. His imaginary scenario goes like this:

You are walking down a street 20 years from now, and a former student recognizes you and rushes up to you. Excitedly, she blurts out: "Oh, it is so good to see you! I was hoping to run into you some day so that I can tell you that I am still writing essays that analyze the author's use of tone. I keep a 'Tone Journal' at home, and I apply that skill you taught me 20 years ago in the tenth grade to everything I read today!" (p. 9)

For Gallagher and most teachers we know, such an encounter with a former student would be nothing less than horrifying. More preferable by far would be finding out that a former student has the confidence, Mojo, and skills to write to a legislator, design a blog, or round up funding for a cause. In any case, it's worth the time to look at what we are offering students and the extent to which the writing we assign has value in the present and the future.

That said, *writing to make an impact* goes beyond an assignment. It involves a whole writing experience. Brooke Ann McWilliams, for instance, takes her Mississippi middle school students on a journey through their tiny community where they can observe with their own eyes what might make their town more attractive and livable. They talk to local officials. They take pictures and make notes in their notebooks. They develop reasons to care about their written proposals. Matt Colley also engages his students in writing about real issues, inviting them to conduct firsthand inquiry (surveys, interviews, focus groups), and once they have developed a plan of action, to pound the pavement with petitions and short pitches. Judy Kennedy asks her students to think back about their experiences with their Make a Living Project, about the challenges of things like buying car insurance and selecting a health care plan and the decisions they made in doing so.

In each of these instances, and in all the other classrooms we have highlighted, the teachers take into account the meaningful destination and, importantly, all the stops along the way.

The idea is to enhance the writing experience so that it will make an impact at some point on any one of these: the student, the teacher, an external audience, a cause. The following considerations are ones we wished we had had in our hip pockets when, at various times in our teaching careers, we were figuring out how to be more expansive, how to do a better job of setting up an experience that mattered to students in the here and now, and might even stand out as meaningful at some later time:

1. In what ways does the writing experience play into kids' curiosity and imagination? Does it make room for the unexpected, the novel, the innovative, the new perspective?
2. How much and what kind of leverage/choice do students have along the way?
3. What is the writing itself supposed to *do*? (Change minds and hearts? Trigger an emotion? Surprise or delight? Turn up the volume?)
4. To what extent is the writing journey connected to making an impact rather than to doing things "correctly"?
5. Who cares? For whom is the writing and the writing experience meaningful? Will it matter to the writer? To an audience? Will it count for something more than a grade?
6. Would you read the writing if you weren't a teacher?
7. What are the chances that students would rate their writing and their writing journey a five on the passion-o-meter?

GETTING STARTED

Be like a postage stamp—stick to one thing until you get there.

—Josh Billings (quoted in Keller, 2013, p. 6)

Multi-tasking is merely the opportunity to screw up more than one thing at a time.

—Steve Uzzell (quoted in Keller, 2013, p. 44)

As these quotes suggest, there is a downside to taking on too much at once. Consider tapering into *writing to make an impact*. No need to shove everything else aside. We offer these ideas for getting started.

Do a Little Audit of Your Writing Tasks

Here's a suggestion for how to go about the audit: Make a date with your curriculum. Grab some snacks. If you like categories, divide your assignments into *yes, no,* or *maybes*. Now, ask yourself a couple of questions about each of the assignments. How much leeway is in each task for students to make some of the decisions—for example, decisions about topic, genre, or process? What is each task intended to do? Does the task give student writers opportunities to make some kind of impact? Can you identify a task that lends itself to *writing to make an impact?*

Review Your Audiences

Let's assume you are the ultimate audience for all the finished projects that cover the surface of your desk or ride on the passenger seat of your car. Where can you invite in other audiences along the way? Do the tasks give students a chance to touch base with others as they work on their projects—for example, to send emails to people in the know to get information, request interviews, or call for action? Recall the Humanitarian Project, the Take Action Project, or the Proteus Project, which connected students digitally with people outside the classroom, whether via email, text, or Instagram. You might scan your favorite writing task for opportunities to share and invite response to your students' work on Google Docs or on public platforms like Change. org, Tumblr, Wattpad, or Teen Ink. In other words, the idea of audience has shifted dramatically from the one we had in the pencil-and-paper days. Now students can (and already do) work in information and social spaces with local and widespread audiences, some of whom may serve as valuable collaborators and supporters.

Pass the Gavel

Part of giving students choice is teaching them how to choose. Where in your curriculum are there pauses when students think with you about how writers create impact, or as Bill Kirby demonstrated on his writing wall, how writers avoid fluff? Consider building in a pause for a real-time model, recommended by Kirby and Gallagher, when you show students how you make decisions about your writing.

At the end of the day, using an applause meter or some other device helps students make judgments about the features of good writing. This, too, is part of passing the gavel—teaching students to recognize which choices work best. (Soon you are going to be clearing the papers off the passenger side of your car.)

Go for Some Passion

Fischer's passion-o-meter offers yet more possibilities. You might recall that Fischer has his students generate lists of topics for the Proteus Project. Picture using the passion-o-meter at the outset to help each student gauge which topics spark the most interest. Once the projects close down, the passion-o-meter becomes part of how students reflect on the personal value of their experience. Was it a five or a three or a one, and why?

Try Out the Idea of Impact

Impact starts with the question: What is this writing supposed to do? Here's how Kelly Gallaher (2011) thinks about an idea like impact:

> Educator Edward Tufte once said, "The point of the essay is to change things." With this in mind, I want to bring my students beyond simply taking a stand and move them into writing that actually proposes solutions. I want their writing to be calls for action, and as such, I want them to convince their readers to *do something*. (pp. 185–186)

Gallagher starts by asking students to write about "five things you can do to. . . ." Examples include: five things you can do to simplify your life, to get healthy, to be more green, to become better at music, dance, swimming, surfing, and on and on. With this opening gamut, Gallaher puts students on the road to writing that has an impact. Consider the point of the writing assignments you give to students. Is it to change things? Remember, too, that the idea of changing things or having an impact is not limited to calls for action in the world. It might be to delight or defuse or distract or some other intention. The road is pretty wide open.

Stick to Impact When Providing Feedback

Instead of using generic rubrics to guide response to writing, stick to the impact of the piece. Generic rubrics focus on features of the writing: organization, mechanics, grammar, diction, sentence structure, and the like. Though there is always room for this kind of feedback, try focusing instead solely on the intended impact. Consider this scenario, adapted from a classroom illustration shared by Grant Wiggins (2009):

1. Ask each writer to provide a draft of his or her paper, whether using Google Docs, digital projector, or old-fashioned paper. Along with the draft, the writer provides an impact statement—a short explanation of what the writer intends for the paper to do. For example: "This entrance essay is supposed to get me into college." "This story is supposed inspire readers to spend less and save more." "This blog is supposed to motivate healthy eating."
2. Ask peer reviewers to give feedback only in terms of impact. Did the writing hit the mark? Highlight places where it succeeds and where it needs beefing up.
3. As an alternative, do not have the writer give away what he or she intended to do. Instead, ask the peer reviewer, after having read the paper, to identify its impact. This is another way for the writer to find out the extent to which his or her writing did what it was supposed to do.

PLAY THE NAME GAME

Naming something has magical powers for learning, remembering, understanding, and analyzing. Whenever and whatever you and your students read—whether mentor texts or student writing—try naming the impact of the piece. Invite lots of responses and discussion. What name or phrases fit best? What is it about the piece that gives it that name?

As a starter kit, you might work from and add to this list of names and phrases we offered throughout this book to describe *writing to make an impact*—writing that exists to do the following:

carry a tune	touch an emotion
change minds and hearts	offer a new perspective
stir up a conversation	make contact
get attention or a laugh	resonate
make a clever point	inspire
shift someone's thinking	move

surprise   propose an idea
convince   entertain
please   enlighten
open a mind   engage
cause a fuss   influence
achieve a feeling   sway
start some kind of thinking   dazzle

LAST BUT NOT LEAST

By "serious" writer who "makes a difference," I don't mean humorless writing about weighty topics, by the way. A serious comedian struggles to craft the joke until it works; if people laugh, you have made a difference. A serious JWT [J. Walter Thompson advertising agency] copywriter hones the ridiculous ad with the talking frog or dancing raisin until it is fresh, fearless—and memorable. (Wiggins, 2009, p. 34)

What's not always fun or rewarding are writing tasks that come off the shelf with the label "Made in school for school purposes only." We are rooting for the kind of writing that goes places, that puts on its marching boots to make something happen, and, by the way, that might even be fun.

It seems to us that this is the exact moment in time for *writing to make an impact*. We have a generation of students in our classrooms who want to make a difference. Most of them know more about social issues, about communicating with audiences, about sharing stories, and about making choices and following a passion than most of us ever did when we were in school. It's not easy to grow up in their world, but it is a world made for doing. We encourage our colleagues to run with the idea of *writing to make an impact* in whatever way will engage your students and support them in finding meaning, learning opportunities, and joy in their writing.

References

Ambrose, S. A., Bridges, M. W., DiPietro, M., Lovett, M. C., & Norman, M. K. (2010). *How learning works.* San Francisco, CA: Jossey Bass.

Anson, C. M., & Beach, R. (1995). *Journals in the classroom: Writing to learn.* Norwood, MA: Christopher-Gordon.

Auster, P. (1994). *City of glass.* New York, NY: Avon Books.

Avi. (1990). *The true confessions of Charlotte Doyle.* New York, NY: Avon Books, Harper Collins.

Barton, D. (2012, December 6). "Real world" writing activities. Retrieved from elt-resourceful.com/2012/12/06/real-world-writing-activities/

Bauer, K. W., & Bennett, J. S. (2003). Alumni perceptions used to assess undergraduate research experience. *The Journal of Higher Education, 74*(2), 210–230. Retrieved from www.tandfonline.com/doi/abs/10.1080/00221546.2003.11777197

Beck, J. (2015, August). Life's stories. *The Atlantic.* Retrieved from www.theatlantic.com/health/archive/2015/08/life-stories-narrative-psychology-redemption-mental-health/400796/

Blakeney, H. (2014, April 16). The miracle of living beyond a deadline. *Laurel Impact,* 14.

Brenna, D. (2010). Sneeze dressing & caribou gravy. In W. Cummins & T. E. Kennedy (Eds.), *The book of worst meals: 25 authors write about terrible culinary experiences.* Serving House Books.

Brooks, R. (2014, December 19). Hashtags explained: The complete guide to hashtags in social media. Retrieved from www.takeflyte.com/hashtags-explained

Camp, R. (1990). Thinking together about portfolios. *The Quarterly of the National Writing Project and the Center for the Study of Writing and Literacy, 12*(2), 8–14.

Caplan, R. (1984). *Writers in training: A guide to developing a composition program for language arts teachers.* Palo Alto, CA: Dale Seymour Publications

Carnegie Corporation and the Center for Information and Research on Civic Learning and Engagement. (2003). Guardian of democracy: The civic mission of schools. Retrieved from civicyouth.org/wp-content/uploads/2011/09/GuardianofDemocracy.pdf

Charles, T. (2008). Poetry for SEN and EAL students. *Making hard topics easier to teach with ICT.* Retrieved from www.englishandict.co.uk/nate/resources/htt.html

Christensen, L. (2009). *Teaching for joy and justice: Re-imagining the language arts classroom.* Milwaukee, WI: Rethinking Schools.

Christensen, L. (2018). Where I'm from: Inviting student lives into the classroom. Retrieved from www.ateq.org/where-im-from-inviting-student-lives-into-the-classroom.html

Christensen, L., & Watson, D. (2015). *Rhythm and resistance: Teaching for joy and justice: Re-imagining the language arts classroom*. Milwaukee, WI: Rethinking Schools.

Cohen, A. (1990, March). Write us an essay, buster and make it interesting—or else. *Wall Street Journal*, 26, p. A1.

College students' commitment to activism, political and civic engagement reach all-time highs. (2016, February 10). *UCLA Newsroom*. Retrieved from newsroom.ucla.edu/releases/college-students-commitment-to-activism-political-and-civic-engagement-reach-all-time-highs

Colley, M. (2017, June 29). Reflections on teaching for civic engagement. Retrieved from www.teachingchannel.org/blog/author/matthewcolley/

Cress, C. M. (2012). Civic engagement and student success: Leveraging multiple degrees of achievement. *Diversity & Democracy, 15*(3). Retrieved from www.aacu.org/publicationsresearch/periodicals/civic-engagement-and-student-success-leveraging-multiple-degrees

Davidson, C. (2017). *The new education: How to revolutionize the university to prepare students for a world in flux*. New York, NY: Basic Books.

Deep learning, surface learning. (1993, April). *AAHE Bulletin 45*(8), 10–13.

De La Paz, S. (2007). Managing cognitive demands for writing: Comparing the effects of instructional components in strategy instruction. *Reading and Writing Quarterly: Overcoming Learning Difficulties, 23*, 249–266.

Delgado, C. (2017). Why civic engagement in the digital age is important [Video file]. Retrieved from www.teachingchannel.org/video/digital-age-civic-engagement-edda

Dellenger, R. (2018). The never-before-told story of Kelly Orgeron, colorful wife to LSU's colorful head coach. Retrieved from www.si.com/college/2018/07/02/kelly-orgeron-lsu-tigers

Denton, P. (2005). *Learning through academic choice*. Turner Falls, MA: Northeast Foundation for Children, Inc.

Dewey, J. (1907). *The school and society.* Chicago, IL: University of Chicago Press.

Donoff, M. (2010). A turbid stew of quivering flotsam. In W. Cummins & T. E. Kennedy (Eds.), *The book of worst meals: 25 authors write about terrible culinary experiences.* Serving House Books.

Dorroh, J. (1993). Reflections on expressive writing in the science class. *The Quarterly, 15*(3), 28–30. Retrieved from www.nwp.org/cs/public/print/resource/1107

Dressman, M., & Genishi, C. (2010). *The essential guide to teaching poetry in a high-stakes, multimodal world.* New York, NY: Teachers College Press.

Eodice, M., Geller, A., & Lerner, N. (2017). *The meaningful writing project: Learning, teaching, and writing in higher education*. Boulder, CO: University Press of Colorado.

Fallows, D. (2014, May 20). Students from Mississippi write about their state. *The Atlantic.* Retrieved from www.theatlantic.com/education/archive/2014/05/student-essays-from-mississippi/371261/

Fox, P. (1998). Inviting dialogue: An alternative to teaching in the dark. *The Clearinghouse, 72*(1), 35–38.

Fulwiler, T., & Young, A. (1982) *Language connections: Writing and reading across the curriculum.* Urbana, IL: National Council of Teachers of English.

Gallagher, K. (2006). *Teaching adolescent writers*, Portland, ME: Stenhouse Publishers.

Gallagher, K. (2011). *Write like this: Teaching real-world writing through modeling & mentor texts.* Portland, ME: Stenhouse Publishers.

Geisel, T. S. (1990). *Oh, the places you'll go!* New York, NY: Random House.

Get rid of the BMI. (n.d.). Retrieved from www.change.org/p/don-get-rid-of-the-bmi

Gladwell, M. (2006, February 13) Million-dollar Murray. *The New Yorker, 25*, 96.

Gladwell, M. (2008). *Outliers: The story of success.* New York, NY: Little, Brown & Company

Goldsmith, M. (2009). *Mojo: How to get it, how to keep it, how to get it back if you lose it.* New York, NY: Hyperion.

Graham, S., Harris, K., & Herbert M. (2011). *Informing writing: The benefits of formative assessment.* Washington, DC: Alliance for Excellent Education. Retrieved from all4ed.org/articles/informing-writing-new-alliance-report-offers-evidence-that -classroom-based-assessments-can-improve-writing-skills-of-american-students/

Graham, S., MacArthur, C., & Fitzgerald, J. (Eds.) (2013). *Best practices in writing instruction* (2nd ed.). New York, NY: Guilford.

Graham, S., & Perin, D. (2007). *Writing next: Effective strategies to improve writing of adolescents in middle and high schools.* New York: Carnegie Corporation.

Guidelines for oral history interviews. (2018). *The History Channel.* Retrieved from images.history.com/images/media/interactives/oralhistguidelines.pdf

Herman, J. (1989). Writing to learn by William Zinsser. *The Quarterly, 11*(3), 16–19. Retrieved from www.nwp.org/cs/public/print/resource/2092

Housden, R. (2011). Why poetry is necessary. Retrieved from www.huffingtonpost.com/ roger-housden/importance-of-poetry_b_884319.html

How civic engagement helps students to see their capacity to make change. (2016). *Mindshift.* Retrieved from www.kqed.org/mindshift/46712/how-civic-engagement -helps-students-see-their-capacity-to-make-change

Howard, K. (1990). Making the writing portfolio real. *The Quarterly, 12*(2), 4–7, 27.

Hughes, J. (2007). *Poetry: A powerful medium for literacy and technology development.* Ontario, Canada: Literacy and Numeracy Secretariat.

I wish I'd been there. (1984). *American Heritage, 36*(1).

Kars, M. (1997). History in a grain of sand: Teaching history and the historian's craft. *The Journal of American History,* 1340–1345.

Keller, G. (2013). *The one thing.* Austin, TX: The Bard Press.

Kent, R. (2014, September). Learning from athletes' writing: Creating activity journals. *English Journal, 104*(1), 68–74.

Knight-Manuel, M. G., & Marciano, J. E. (2018). *Classroom cultures: Equitable schooling for racially diverse youth.* New York, NY: Teachers College Press

Ladson-Billings, G. (1995). But that's just good teaching! The case for culturally relevant pedagogy. *Theory into Practice. 34*(3), 159-165.

Lang, J. M. (2017, November 15). Will they remember writing it? *Chronicle of Higher Education.* Retrieved from www.chronicle.com/article/Will-They-Remember -Writing-It-/241657

LeMahieu, P. G., Gitomer, D. H., & Eresh, J. A. (1995). Portfolios in large-scale assessment: Difficult but not impossible. *Educational Measurement: Issues and Practices 14*(3), 11–28.

Leslie, I. (2014). *Curious: The desire to know and why your future depends on it.* New York, NY: Basic Books.

Levstik, L., & Barton., K. (1997). *Doing history: Investigating with children in elementary and middle schools.* Mahwah, NJ: Lawrence Erlbaum Associates.

Lindblom, K. (2015, July 27). School writing vs. authentic writing. *Teachers, profs, parents: Writers who care.* Retrieved from writerswhocare.wordpress.com/2015/07/27/school-writing-vs-authentic-writing/

Lovell, J. (2013, July 31). The 6th floor. *The New York Times Magazine.* Retrieved from 6thfloor.blogs.nytimes.com/2013/07/31/george-saunderss-advice-to-graduates/?_php=true&_type=blogs&_r=0

Lunsford, A. (2011). *St. Martin's Handbook* (7th ed.). Boston, MA: Bedford/St. Martin's.

Mayher, J. S., Lester, N., & Pradl, G. (1983). *Learning to write/writing to learn.* Portsmouth, NH: Heinemann

McGriff, M. (2015). The image list: Starting with images rather than words can help show an experience, instead of telling it. *The Poetry Foundation.* Retrieved from www.poetryfoundation.org/articles/70291/the-image-list

Meltzer, L. (2010). *Promoting executive function in the classroom.* New York, NY: The Guilford Press.

Middaugh, E. (2015). Supporting school engagement in Oakland high schools. Retrieved from eddaoakland.org/wp-content/uploads/2015/06/EDDA_Research_Student-Engagement_030715.pdf

Murphy, S., & Smith, M. (2015). *Uncommonly good ideas: Teaching writing in the common core era.* New York, NY: Teachers College Press.

Murray, D. (2013). *The craft of revision* (5th ed.). Boston, MA: Wadsworth.

National Research Council. (2000, September). *How people learn: Brain, mind, experience, and school* (expanded ed.). Washington, DC: National Academies Press.

National Writing Project & Nagin, C. (2006). *Because writing matters.* San Francisco, CA: John Wiley & Sons.

Newkirk, T. N. (2014), *Minds made for stories: How we really read and write informational and persuasive texts.* Portsmouth, NH: Heinemann.

Nguyen, B. M. (2007). *Stealing Buddha's dinner.* London, England: Penguin Books.

O'Connell, M. J., & Vandas, K. L. (2016) How to increase student investment in learning. Retrieved from corwin-connect.com/2016/08/increase-student-investment-learning/

Pekar, H., & Buhle, P. (2009). *Studds Terkel's working: A graphic adaptation.* New York, NY: The New Press.

Pesick, S. (1998, November). *Reading, writing, and history: Teaching for historical thinking and understanding* (Unpublished doctoral dissertation). Stanford University. UMI Number 9837135.

Pesick, S. (2001a). Writing history: Portfolios, student perspective, and historical understanding. In M. A. Smith & J. Juska (Eds.), *The whole story: Teachers talk about portfolios* (pp. 129–145). Berkeley, CA: National Writing Project.

Pesick, S. (2001b). *Reading, writing, and history: Teaching for historical thinking and understanding.* Unpublished manuscript.

Pesick, S. (2019). How the "fly on the wall" changed my teaching. Presentation at the Fourth Annual Forum of the Bay Area Writing Project, University of California, Berkeley, CA.

Pollan, M. (2007). *Omnivore's dilemma: The search for a perfect meal in a fast-food world.* London, England: Bloomsbury.

Rampolla, M. L. (2017). *A pocket guide to writing in history* (9th ed.). New York, NY: Bedford/St. Martins.

Rankine, C. (2004). "At the airport-security checkpoint . . ." *Don't let me be lonely: An American lyric.* St. Paul, MN: Graywolf Press.

Reed, S. (1988). Logs: Keeping an open mind. *English Journal, 77*(2).

Reichl, R. (1998). *Tender at the bone.* New York, NY: Random House.

Rice, B. (2013, April 30). Write to think. Retrieved from medium.com/@billrice/write-to-think-37ed8038b1ec

Richardson, E. (2014). *The pizazz factor: Writing successful college-application essays.* Unpublished manuscript. Columbus, MS: The Mississippi School for Mathematics and Science.

Rose, A. (2017). *The ready-made thief.* New York, NY: Viking.

Saul, S. (2018, June 3). The story behind this site: Or, can a lecture course also be a publication workshop? Retrieved from theseventies.berkeley.edu/godfather/2018/06/03/the-story-behind-this-site-or-can-a-lecture-course-also-be-a-publication-workshop/

Simmons, A. (2014). Why poetry is so important: The oft-neglected literary form can help students learn in ways that prose can't. *The Atlantic.* Retrieved from www.theatlantic.com/education/archive/2014/04/why-teaching-poetry-is-so-important/360346/.

Simmons, R. (2018, October 29). Cal stuns no. 15 Washington with a 12-10 upset. *SFGATE.* Retrieved from www.sfgate.com/collegesports/article/Cal-stuns-No-15-Washington-with-a-12-10-upset-13342347.php

Smith, A. M. (2010). Poetry performances and academic identity negotiations in the literacy experiences of seventh-grade language arts students. *Reading Improvement, 47*(4), 202–218.

Smith, M. A. (1993) Introduction: Portfolio classrooms. In M. A. Smith & M. Ylivisaker (Eds.), *Teachers' voices: Portfolios in the classroom* (pp.1–9). Berkeley, CA: National Writing Project.

Soldiers' stories. (2006, June 12). *New Yorker.* Retrieved from www.newyorker.com/magazine/2006/06/12/soldiers-stories

Soltis, J. F. (1994). Foreword. In R. L. Hopkins, *Narrative schooling: Experiential learning and the transformation of American education* (p. xi). New York, NY: Teachers College Press.

Spencer, J. (2018). Five structures for helping students learn about project management. Retrieved from www.spencerauthor.com/project-management/

Sterling, R. (2006, November 17) Writing for a change. NWP annual meeting speech. Retrieved from www.nwp.org/cs/public/print/resource/2366?x-print_friendly=1

Stop sexual assault in Oakland Unified School District. (2017). Retrieved from www.change.org/p/interim-superintendent-devin-dillon-stop-sexual-assault-in-oakland-unified-school-district

Taczak, K., & Robertson, L. (2016). Reiterative reflection in the twenty-first-century writing classroom: An integrated approach to teaching for transfer. In K. Yancey (Ed.), *A rhetoric of reflection* (pp. 42–63). Boulder, CO: Utah State University Press.

Taylor, C., & Dewsbury, B. M. (2018). On the problem and promise of metaphor use in science and science communication. *Journal of Microbiology & Biology Education, 19*(1). Retrieved from www.ncbi.nlm.nih.gov/pmc/articles/PMC5969428/ doi:10.1128/jmbe.v19i1.1538

Terkel, S. (1997). *Working: People talk about what they do all day and how they feel about what they do.* New York, NY: The New Press.

Tierney, R. (1981). Using expressive writing to teach biology. In A. Wotring & R. Tierney, *Two studies of writing in high school science* (pp. 47–69). Berkeley, CA: University of California, Bay Area Writing Project.

Von Stumm, S., Hell, B., & Chamorro-Premuzic, T. (2011). The hungry mind: Intellectual curiosity is the third pillar of academic performance. *Perspectives on Psychological Science, 6*(6), 574, 588.

Warner, J. (2018) *Why they can't write: Killing the five-paragraph essay and other necessities,* Baltimore, MD: Johns Hopkins University Press.

Whitney, A. E. (2011, October). In search of the authentic English classroom: Facing the schoolishness of school. *English Education, 44*(1), 51–62.

Wiggins, G. (2009). Real-world writing: Making purpose and audience matter. *English Journal, 98*(5), 29–37.

Xerri, D. (2012). Poetry teaching and multimodality: Theory into practice. *Creative Education, 3*(4), 507–512.

Yancey, K. B. (1998). *Reflection in the writing classroom.* Logan, UT: Utah State University Press.

Yancey, K. B. (2009). *Writing in the 21st century: A report from NCTE.* Retrieved from www.ncte.org/library/NCTEFiles/Press/Yancey_final.pdf

Yancey, K. B., Robertson, L., & Taczak, K. (2014). *Writing across contexts: Transfer, composition, and sites of writing.* Logan, UT: Utah State University Press.

Zemelman, S. (2016). *From inquiry to action: Civic engagement with project-based learning in all content areas.* Portsmouth, NH: Heinemann.

Zemelman, S. (2017, May 18). Guest post: Ideas for civic action in a time of social uncertainty. *The New York Times.* Retrieved from www.nytimes.com/2017/05/18/learning/lesson-plans/guest-post-ideas-for-student-civic-action-in-a-time-of-social-uncertainty.html

Index

The letter *f* following a page number indicates a figure.

About the Authors

Sandra Murphy is professor emerita at the University of California, Davis, where she also directed the Center for Cooperative Research and Extension Services for Schools and acted as faculty advisor to the Area 3 Writing Project. Her publications include *Designing Writing Tasks for the Assessment of Writing* (with Leo Ruth); *Writing Portfolios: A Bridge from Teaching to Assessment* (with Mary Ann Smith); *Portfolio Practices: Lessons from Schools, Districts, and States* (with Terry Underwood); *Assessment for Learning: Using Rubrics to Improve Student Writing*, a K–5 book series (with Sally Hampton and Margaret Lowery); and *Uncommonly Good Ideas: Teaching Writing in the Common Core Era* (with Mary Ann Smith). She cochaired the Steering Committee of NAEP to develop the 2011 framework for the National Assessment of Educational Progress in Writing. While serving as a work group member to develop the Common Core State Standards, she coauthored the standards for writing with Sally Hampton. According to Murphy, all of her work is informed by the years she spent teaching high school and community college literature and composition.

Mary Ann Smith directed the Bay Area and California Writing Projects and served as director of government relations and public affairs for the National Writing Project. She is coauthor (with Sandra Murphy) of *Writing Portfolios: A Bridge from Teaching to Assessment,* coeditor (with Miriam Ylvisaker) of *Teachers' Voices: Portfolios in the Classroom,* coeditor (with Jane Juska) of *The Whole Story: Teachers Talk About Portfolios,* coauthor (with Sandra Murphy) of *Uncommonly Good Ideas: Teaching Writing in the Common Core Era,* and coauthor (with Sherry Seale Swain) of *Assessing Writing, Teaching Writers: Putting the Analytic Writing Continuum to work in Your Classroom.* According to Smith, everything important she knows about writing is thanks to her many years teaching middle and high school students and to the thousands of great teachers and colleagues she has worked with around the country through the Writing Project.